PANTHER

PANTHER

ISBN: 978-91-976773-5-6

Project manager & Art director: Toni Canfora
Project supervisor: Roddy MacDougall, Mirko Bayerl
Translation: Roddy MacDougall, Johan Augustsson
Print: Ljungbergs Tryckeri, Klippan, Sweden

Canfora Grafisk Form & Förlag
Bondesonsgatan 4
112 52 Stockholm - Sweden
info@canfora.se - www.canfora.se

FOREWORD

It is a great honour to introduce this exciting Panther book. During the past forty years I have been author of many technical books about the Panther. In these books I have, with my colleagues, worked hard to research the development and combat history of the Panther. Through my drawings I have set out the changes that occurred during the period from 1942 to 1945.

The Authors of this book have now brought together their knowledge, experience and skills to animate the story of the Panther and give an insight into how specific Panthers served especially in the desperate defensive battles of 1944 and 1945.

Many modellers invest time and skills in their models. The authors of this book have moved many steps beyond the demands of model making. Each chapter of this book demonstrates a piece of history which is supported by extensive research not only on the technical aspects of the Panther in question but also wide and deep historical research. The result of each project should be a great inspiration to others when undertaking their own modelling projects and encourage them to read-up on their subject in order to make the result more realistic.

The spread of Panthers in this book covers all the major versions. Ausf.D, Ausf.A and several versions of the Ausf.G including ones prepared for Infrared equipment, Befehlspanther and Panther Ausf.G with Steel tyred road wheels are all featured.

The geographical coverage is very wide and includes the Ardennes, Italy, Poland, Estonia and several articles on those desperate and futile battles in Hungary 1945. Having carried out research in many battlefields I am always amazed at the talent that is needed to track down specific locations and then take photos that show the current setting for the actions that took place 60 years ago. The finding of original items that still show the colour schemes of specific Panthers is a very worthwhile venture.

A great collection of period photos have been selected to support the research on each vehicle. I look forward to further research and models from the team in the future.

Hilary Louis Doyle
March 2011

INTRODUCTION

Dear reader, You hold in your hands the result of a modelling adventure that started some two years ago when group of modellers set out to model the Panther Ausf.G tank. Initially this was a group build where the modellers shared the process of the build and their knowledge of the Panther tank. The models background were to be thoroughly researched to determine the unit, location, production date etc.

Initially I was not involved in this group but when I heard about it I realised the models could be used to make an interesting book. After discussions with Mirko Bayerl and Roddy MacDougall as well as the modellers involved in the group build, I decided to go ahead with this project and turn their work into a book. I also decided that I wanted to include models of the Panther Ausf. A and Ausf. D, fortunately it did not take me too long to round up some further crew members for the book who were eager to participate.

I would not go as far as saying this book is unique, or that the quality of the models are higher than in other publications, but I believe we have managed to connect modelling and history in a way that is not commonly seen. The book should not be seen as a build guide to the Panther tank, but rather as a source of inspiration and I hope it will encourage modellers to connect their models to the history that surrounds them and encourage them to build their models as accurately as they are able to. There are so many talented modellers on the scene today, each day we see fantastic new models in magazines and on Internet forums. The models that really give an extra kick are those where the modellers have put their souls into the project, incorporating their research to recreate a historically correct model set in the correct environment.

I believe that we have managed to depict an interesting mix of Panthers in this book, from the Ausf. D to late Ausf. G´s, from North to South and East to West. Each one with their own story to tell. I hope that some of the information presented in the various articles is new to many and can help bring some questions into a new light.

This book would obviously not have been possible to produce without the participation of the modellers whose work is presented in it and I would like to express my gratitude for the passion and commitment they have put into their models.

I could not have produced this book without the help and supervision of Roddy MacDougall and Mirko Bayerl. Their knowledge about the Panther tank and their deployment is exceeded by very few. Furthermore, they have been a link between the modellers involved and also provided invaluable help when obtaining many of the photos seen in this book, some of which are being published for the first time.

Finally, I would also like to thank the following people who have assisted us with historical background, photos and technical information:

Martin Block, Hilary Doyle, Lee Archer, Mike Wood, Peti Barnaky, István Tóth, Kamen Nevenkin and in particular Otto Jozsa whose help was invaluable.

Toni Canfora, editor & publisher

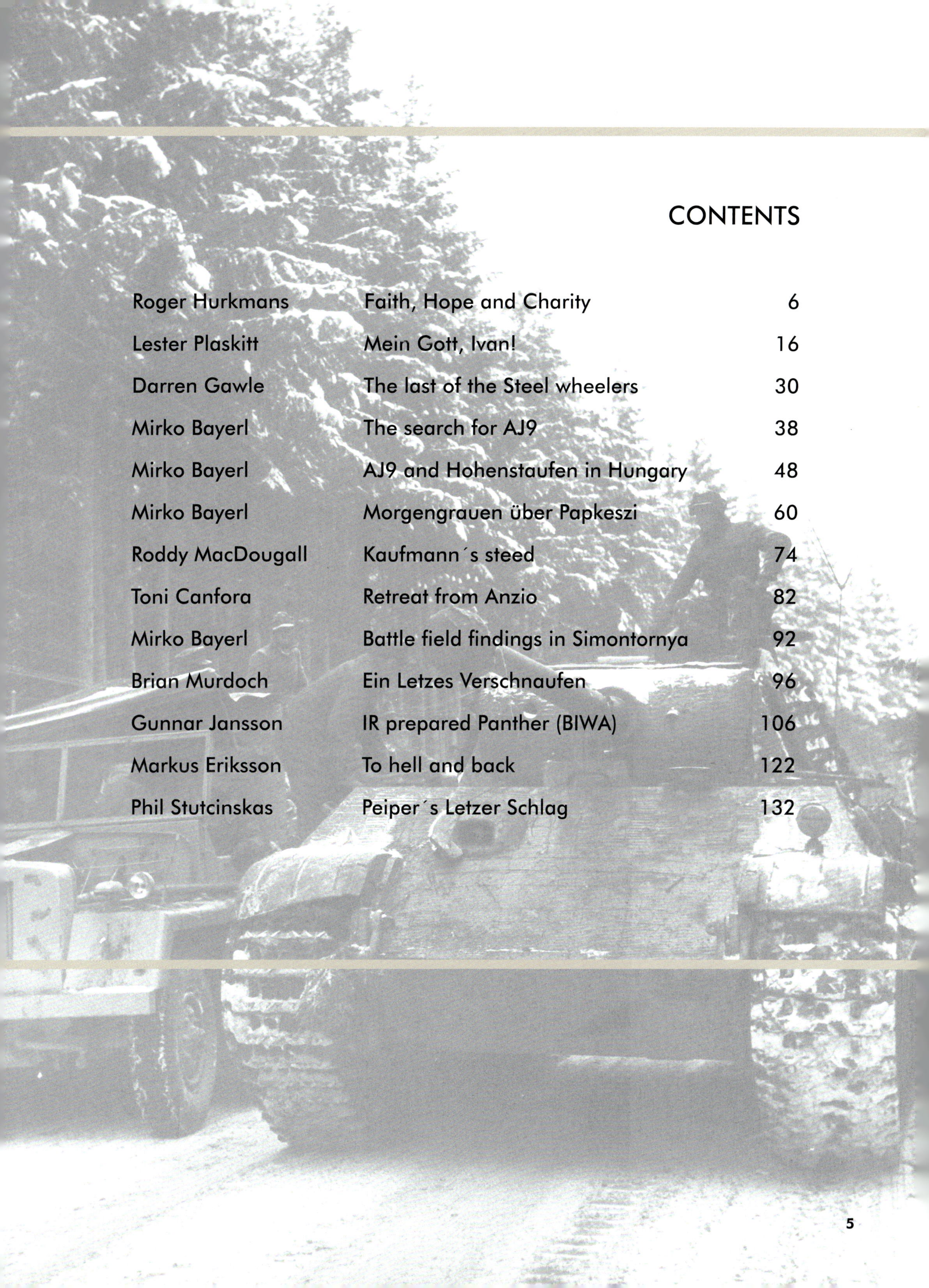

CONTENTS

FAITH, HOPE

FINLAND
Helsinki
Gulf of Finland
Narva
Tallinn
ESTONIA
Lake Peipus
Tartu
Pärnu
Saaremaa
Hiiumaa
Gulf of Riga
RUSSIA
Pskov
Valmiera
Cēsis
LATVIA
Riga
Ventspils
Liepāja
Jelgava
Daugavpils
Rēzekne
Šiauliai
Panevėžys
LITHUANIA
Klaipėda

11. SS Panzer Abteilung "Hermann von Salza", Narwa, 1944

AND CHARITY

Dutch modeller Roger Hurkmans decided to portray a battle weary Panther Ausf. D from the legendary and rarely photographed unit 11. SS Pz. Abteilung "Hermann von Salza". This unit operated in conjunction with 11. Freiwilligen Pz.Gren.Div. "Nordland". An assembly of converted stock figures makes up the crew of his vignette, depicting a moment frozen in history.

By the end of March 1943 Hitler gave the order to set up the new III.SS-Pz.Corps and at the same time most of the Dutch and some of the Scandinavian volunteers serving within the SS were taken from the frontline units they were serving with to reorganize.

Most of the Scandinavians volunteers were assigned to the Nordland Division and the majority of Dutch volunteers were given their own independent brigade but not in the Nordland. This was mainly due to political influence from the Netherlands. The link between Nordland and Nederland was that both fought as Germanic volunteers on the Eastern front as well as on the Northern front.

The Korps was commanded by of one of the best known Waffen-SS generals, Generalmajor of the Waffen-SS, Felix Steiner, who was given command because of his experience with foreign volunteers. The composition and history of the Panzer Regiment is interesting, there were several changes to its structure and the equipment that was eventually issued. On 22.3.1943 the initial formation orders for the SS-Pz.Gren. Div. 'Nordland' authorized an SS-Pz.Rgt. with seven Panzer companies. The I. Abt. Would be equipped with two light (Pz. III), one medium (Pz. IV) and one heavy (Pz. VI) companies. The II. Abt. Was to consist of two light (Pz. III) and one medium (Pz. IV) companies. A revised order was issued on 28.6.1943 authorizing a SS-Pz.Rgt. with eight Panzer companies, split into four medium companies equipped with Panthers (Pz. V) in both the I. Abt. And the II. Abt.

After it had become clear that Panther production would struggle to fully equip the existing Panzer units from both the Heer and Waffen-SS, a new order was

Note the worn off whitewash especially on the front where the crew climbs on and off.

issued on the 30.10.43 stating that the composition of Pz.Rgt. for SS-Pz.Gren. Div. 'Nordland' would be downsized to either a Pz.(Stu.Gesch.)Abt. with three StuG companies or four Pz. IV companies, depending on the resources available. This structure was how the Panzer regiment was supposed to have been equipped and organised. It was intended that SS-Pz.Abt. 11 was never meant to have been equipped with Panthers after this point, however, they got some by chance in the end but we will come back to this!

While all of this had been going on H.Gr. Süd had provided sixty five M 42 tanks and fifteen L6 assault guns from captured Italian stocks to units from III. SS-Pz.Korps. SS-Pz.Abt. 11 received an unknown number of them for training purposes and used them in anti-partisan operations. At the beginning of November 1943, Hitler demanded that sixty of the Panther from the mechanically unreliable first production series of Panther D's, were to be sent to the 'Oranienbaumer Kessel' and placed in static positions along the German front line in order to strengthen the anti-tank defences there. These Panthers were to be taken from the seventy one that were issued to I./SS-Pz.Rgt. 1 in June and July 1943, but were quickly declared as unsuitable for active frontline service. The sixty Panthers, with a small escort command

The spare tracks where also treated with the hairspray technique only this time it was sprayed with the yellow base colour.

The bicycle could be used by the crewmembers for short distance. It is the Tamiya kit and was detailed using an Aber PE set.

Collection Mirko Bayerl

One of the Panther Ausf D's used by Hermann von Salza in the Narva area.

Collection Mirko Bayerl

Since the Panthers from Herman von Salsa had so many technical problems, a few recovery T34's where added to the abteilung.

Collection Mirko Bayerl

A knocked out Panther Ausf. D of II Abt. Herman von Salsa.

were shipped from the Magdeburg-Königsborn ordnance depot to H.Gr. Nord between the 5th and 25th November1943. These Vehicles were taken over by units under L. (50th) A.K. which consisted of 9. and 10. Lw.Feld-Div. along with K.Gr. 4. SS-Pol.Pz.Gren.Div. at that time. Most of the Panthers were immobile and thus they were dug in to fixed positions with only the turret showing above ground. A few the Panthers that were still mobile were kept behind the front lines for training drivers.

H.Gr. soon reported trouble in providing enough trained anti-tank personnel to operate the sixty Panthers. The Gen. Insp.d.Pz.Tr. decideded to send sixty crews from I./Pz.Rgt. 29 who were then under conversion to Panthers in Germany, to the 'Oranienbaumer Kessel'. Each crew consist of just three men, a commander, gunner and driver. Since there were no plans to build the sixty Panthers into a fully mobile unit, only a minimum maintenance unit was provided. Drivers were only there to move the tanks between pre-arranged dug-in positions in case of emergency.

The men of I./29 transfer to the area in late November 1943. They managed to keep about one company of Panthers mobile with great difficulty, while the bulk of the remaining Panthers were in fixed positions.

On 12th December 1943 the III.(germ.) SS-Pz.Korps arrived from Croatia and took over responsibility at the 'Oranienbaumer Kessel'. The 'Nordland' Div. and "Nederland" Brig. moved in between the 9. and 10. Lw.Feld-Div. where they took over parts of their former sectors on the front. The dug-in Panthers with I./29 crews remained in place in the various divisional sectors. SS-Pz. Abt. 11 initially remained in Croatia where they were still waiting to be equipped with Sturmgeschutz.

Following a request by III.(germ) SS-Pz.Korps Crews to A.O.K , eighteen crews from SS-Pz.Abt. 11 finally arrived in the 'Oranienbaumer Kessel' on the 30th December 1943. It was planned to equip them with 45 StuG in the H.Gr. Nord area as soon as possible, but as it turned out this never happened. During the following weeks the bulk of the unit were used as infantry, providing security in less threatened sectors of the front. A handful of SS-crews manned some of the I./29 Panthers that were dug-in on the sectors of 'Nordland' and 'Nederland' front in January 1944. The exact figures are hard to establish, but it seems that 'Nordland' had about 5 dug-in and immobile Panthers in its sector at best.

The Russian offensive on the 'Oranienbaumer Kessel' began on the 14th January 1944 and most of the dug-in Panthers along the front were lost as a result of this. Some were destroyed by the enemy but most had to be abandoned when the German units retreated.

Only 14 out of the originally sixty Panther D's made it back to the German held Narwa Bridghead. The I./29 wass ordered to had all of the remaining 14 Panthers to SS-Pz. Abt. 11 on the 12th February 1944 and then return to France. Although this order speaks of thirteen Panthers, other records indicate that it was possibly fourteen Panthers that were handed over. These remained the only Panthers that 1./SS-Pz.Abt. 11 ever

UPDATES OF THE KIT

1. Aber barrel.
2. Aber fenders, brackets, toolholders etc.
3. Aber side skirts.
4. Cleaning rods from brass tubing.
5. Tube for cleaning rods made from lead foil.
6. Modelkasten tracks.

received during the war! Despite the fact that some post war books repeatedly say otherwise, German records show that there were no replacement Panthers issued at all, the thirteen or fourteen old Panther Ausf. D's, taken over from the I./29 were the only Panthers that SS-Pz.Abt. 11 ever received..

Panther D construction

The Ausf.D was the initial production model of the Panther. It was based on the versuchs series and the first 20 vehicles had 21 litre engines, clutch and brake steering, a large bulge in the left turret side for the cupola and a 60 mm glacis plate. Subsequent Panthers had an 80mm thick glacis, and the turret was re designed, a 23 litre engine was also installed along with a new epicyclical steering that greatly improved manoeuvrability. I used the excellent Dragon Panther Ausf D as a basis for this project and I chose Aber's extensive upgrade set (AB35K02) which includes everything you need from their various aftermarket sets i.e. schurtzen, front fenders, stowage bins, engine grilles, gun barrel, cables and other general updates.

For the tracks I have chosen to use Modelkasten early tracks. The only problem with these tracks is that you have to thin down the rear idler wheel a bit to make them fit.

The cleaning rod tube was made from lead foil taken from the neck of a champagne bottle. It is thin, easy to roll and it can be damaged to the desired extent using a small screwdriver or a sharp object. I used copper rod to make the cleaning rods.

Painting the Panther

I first airbrushed the Panther with a deep dark warm brown colour. To build up the contrast I first used a dark sand colour that was followed by subsequently lighter shades of yellow. I angled the airbrush so that the colour stuck mainly to the raised areas, leaving a shadow from the darker base coat underneath. This was followed by a even lighter colour to create further variety and highlights. Now the vehicle was sprayed with Citadel gloss varnish to protect the paint before the weathering process. The left over white wash was achieved by first spraying the vehicle with hairspray and then white paint was applied in a random pattern on the model. After that, you can easily remove sections of the white with a stiff brush and warm water.

Then the weathering process can begin. I used a mix of dark oils for weathering, filtering and outlining the vehicle. For chips and scrapes on the paintwork I always use acrylic paint, heavily diluted with water, as this paints can be applied in very thin lines. I find the chipping an essential stage in realistic weathering, but this should never be exaggerated. The tracks were painted dark grey and weathered with pigments. This was done with a base of water because the modelkasten tracks are made of plastic and the plastic small pins can melt if white spirit or certain thinners are used and then

A complete view from the tank and base. The figures where integrated to the Panther by re sculpting the contact area with magic-sculpt, giving a feeling of a natural "sit".

you have a loose set of tracks again! As a final step I dry brushed the tracks with black to add depth to their appearance.

To simulate the mud on the Panther I first added some texture with fine sand mixed with diluted Tamiya putty. After spraying the Panther in its base colour I painted the mud with van dijck brown oil paint. It is important to blend the mud colour into the base colour. After this the boogie wheels where weathered with pigment powders. On the back of the Panther I spattered some diluted raw umber and van dijck brown oil paint to represent wet mud.

Building and painting the figures

At the beginning of this project, I decided that I wanted the pose of the figures to be as natural as possible. I then set about selecting the figures and parts of figures I would use. Most of what I ended up using consisted of plastic figures from Dragon. It was a question of placing various arms and legs in place, then filling the gaps and re sculpting using Magic sculp. I went in search of replacement heads and hands, almost all of which come from Hornet. The little boy was nearly out of the box and comes from the Russian manufacturer Zelenkov.

I painted both the uniforms and faces with oils. If you use oils, I recommend that you start off with a good base coat of acrylic or enamel paint. This method works best if your undercoats are approximately the same colour as the oils. I let the undercoat dry for at least a day before I began working with

the oils. I first add the base colour, followed by the shadow, in general van dijck brown. I always paint the lower parts of the arms in a slightly darker shade to accentuate the shadows. The highlight colour was done by adding some white to the base colour and applying it to the raised areas on the figures. Oil paints are excellent for weathering uniforms and blending in dirt tones to the uniforms colours. Another advantage of oil paints is that they dry slowly, giving you a lot more time to achieve the look you desire. The disadvantage of course, is that you have to wait a couple of days for the figure to dry. Once everything was completely dry, both figures and model, I airbrushed them with a coat of matt varnish to get rid of the sheen that is a characteristic of oil paints. I used Archer transfers for the uniform patches. The final step is weathering the lower parts of the uniform trousers, the boots and the helmets using MIG pigments.

The Base

The wooden base was made by a Dutch firm that is specialises in making bases to order. I cut a piece of Styrofoam that was treated with a gap filler and fixed it to the base plate. Fine sand mixed with diluted wood glue was added to the base. After airbrushing several layers of brown colours, the snow was added. I used potato starch for this and the icy snow was a commercial product from Deluxe materials. As a final touch I glued a nameplate onto the wooden base. I always get my nameplates from the UK based firm "Name-it" and these add a classy finishing touch!

Conclusion

This was my third diorama where I did more research on the background and history from the vehicle I wanted to build and I must admit that I enjoy these projects more. Modellers spend a lot of money on aftermarket sets so why not spend more time and money on references. It gives you more inspiration and brings you closer to "reality".

I want to thank Jan Willem Stokkers for his support, Peter Klink for taking the photos and Martin Block for finally providing the correct information regarding the formation and composition of SS-Pz.Abt. 11.

Roger Hurkmans

Biography

Martin Block's private archive and research collection

Tragedy of the Faithful by Wihellm Tieke

Nederlandse Vrijwilligers in Europese krijgsdienst 1940-1945 part 3

KTB from Brigade and Division Nederland Freiburg Militaire Archive

316
"Faith, Hope and Charity"
11.SS.Panzer Abteilung "Hermann von Salza"
11.SS.Freiwilligen Panzer Grenadiers "Nordland"
Narwa February 1944

Panther Ausf. G, 23 Panzer Divison, Hungary 1945

MEIN GOTT, IVAN!

Lester Plaskitt found inspiration for his Panther project in a series of war time photos along with a thorough historical background. When finishing the model he even used soil from the actual road strip where his subject was photographed some 65 years ago.

I find the inspiration for a model is often found in a particular period photograph, which sparks an interest in the subject, be it the moment in time the photograph captures or some detail in the subject of the photo. This is what happened to me when I came across a picture of a Panther G, apparently abandoned on an unfinished road somewhere in Hungary, during the latter stages of World War II. What really caught my eye was the two rolls of spare tracks coiled up on the engine deck, my first thoughts were what an excellent subject for a model. Of course, I could have modelled the vehicle as depicted in the photograph, abandoned on the roadside but then I began to think, why has it been abandoned? It had evidence of damage to the turret with Russian investigation numbers painted on, had that damage been what had knocked the tank out? But what my mind kept coming back too was why did it have the tracks on the engine deck, I did not think they were there to serve as anti aircraft protection as they would have been impossible to remove for the everyday maintenance of the vehicle also due to their positioning it would have been very difficult to refuel the Panther, these points coupled with the fact that driving with this extra weight would add extra stress to an already overstressed engine and gearbox made me think they must have been placed there for a different reason. With this in mind, I approached Mirko Bayerl who is well known for his extensive knowledge of the late Hungarian war campaign, after talking with Mirko he agreed to carry out research on my behalf as to the story behind his particular vehicle.

The story begins with the Panther itself, being built in the September/October production batch by Daimler Benz, this infra red (IR) enabled Panther was issued to I.Abt Pz. Lehr Rgt. 130 which was dispatched to Hungary in December 1944 as an independent battalion (with the mixed regiments other battalion fighting in the Ardennes offensive) partly attached to 1. Pz. Div. during the first weeks of fighting then becoming part of Panzergruppe Pape, until the battalion was recalled back to Germany in January 1945 where it was to be re equipped with new vehicles. Before its departure, the unit handed over its remaining Panthers, with 37 Panthers going to 1. Pz. Div. and 11 Panthers to the 23. Pz. Div. to replace vehicle losses (note that although most of the Panthers handed over were IR capable there was no IR equipment with them as Panzer Lehr had not taken any of this equipment to Hungary). Upon receiving the Panthers 23. Pz.Div, they carried out some field modifications, which included adding spare track hangers to the turret, which allowed lengths of spare track to the hang on the turret sides to act as extra amour. After hard fighting through out the freezing Hungarian winter and mud choked spring thaw, this Panther, by March 1945 had found itself, we believe due to engine problems, in the large maintenance depot set up as a central repair centre for all German and Hungarian forces in Hungary outside the village of Hajmasker, which was a large training and repair base used by the Hungarian army. The Germans had chosen to use this depot as it boasted excellent workshop facilities and good rail links that enabled replacement vehicles, spare parts and supplies to be easily shipped from the Reich. The German forces in Hungary, in March 1945, faced a desperate situation after the failure of the Spring awakening offensive. The depleted forces could offer no effective cohesive defence structure, most of the resistance to the on coming Russian hoards

Taken in 1945 a view from the front of the column of abandoned vehicles showing a Zwischenlosung at the head of the line with the Panthers behind heading towards the village of Szentkiralyszabadja, note the details of the then unfinished road.

Collection Mirko Bayerl

The column of vehicles taken from the right-hand side of the road, three of the Panthers are facing backwards indicating they may have been under tow? The subject of the model can just be seen, it is the 5th Panther in the line.

AMC

An amazing comparison photo showing the exact same road strip today. Note the hills and electrical poles in the background enabling the indentification.

March 1945 looking down the column of Panthers from a position behind the Zwischenlosung showing to good advantage the width of the road and the depth of the ditches on either side. Note the ausf A model at the front of the line of Panthers.

AMC

lay with small battle groups of a few tanks and armoured vehicles that were fighting individual holding engagements until either their ammunition or fuel ran out or they were simply outflanked by the advancing Russian tank armies, other units were in headlong flight trying to reach the Western allies lines in the attempt to surrender and escape the wrath of the Red Army. Around the 20th of March the Russian steamroller, advancing towards Austria and Vienna had reached the outskirts of Hajmasker causing widespread panic amongst the maintenance personnel and tank crews still in the repair depot. A hasty decision was make to try and evacuate Hajmasker taking any of the vehicles that could be salvaged along with any usable spares and equipment and try to retreat along main road number 8 towards Veszprem (which at that time was being defended by elements of the LAH SS under the command of Jochen Peiper and later the 3. Pz. Div.) and eventually reach allied lines. The war diary of 23. Pz. Rgt. tells us that during the night two disabled Panthers, that had been dug in on the outskirts of Hajmasker for the defence of the repair depot, were destroyed by there crews and a small convoy of vehicles consisting of several Panthers all with mechanical problems, (some being able to move under there own power and others being towed) a number of other armoured vehicles including some recovery vehicles including Bergepanther and various other vehicles all loaded with as much vital equipment as could be carried to keep the vehicles running or would help in the canalisation of spare parts from any of the vehicles that broke down limped out of Hajmasker in an attempt to reach safety.

Making painfully slow progress, the convoy of vehicles had managed to reach a side road coming off main road number 8, Hungarian engineers using some elements of slave labour to connect the main number

A direct modern day comparrison photograph showing the exact location of where the subject Panther stood on the road in 1945, with details of the adjacent ditch still evedent despite the encroaching vegitation. Note that the location of the modern electrical pole in the background is the same as in the war time photo.

The subject vehicle as depicted in the model showing details such as the coiled track on the engine deck and the distinctive armoured stowage box mounted on the right hand side of the rear hull for the IR optical equipment, though this equipment was not deployed in Hungary with I.Abt Pz. Lehr Rgt 130.

Max K. via Mirko Bayerl

8 road to a military airfield outside of Veszperm, close to the small village of Szentkiralyszabadja, had built this road in 1942. The road had not been fully finished, as, although having large ditches on either side of the road to catch drifting snow and keep the road clear, it did not have a finished surface. At this time, the surface was made up of compacted chalky coloured dolomite. It is at this point in the story I decided to portray my Panther, with the crew noticing vehicles in the distance and realising that Ivan had begun to catch up with them. One can only imagine the feelings of the fleeing Germans, exhausted with the ever present threat of the advancing Russians catching them, praying their vehicles would be able to keep going long enough to enable an escape, not wanting to think what the nightmare of being taken prisoner by the dreaded Ivan may entail. No one for sure knows what happened when the Russians caught up with the convoy, the general opinion is that when the crews saw the Russians approaching from the East and North East they quickly abandoned any of the vehicles that could not move with any degree of speed and continued their flight on the remaining serviceable vehicles, with some of the crew attempting to destroy their vehicles as was the German army doctrine, others simply trying to make their escape on foot. There is a record in a book published

A close up of the damage caused to Panther number 74 which stood in line directly infront of my subject Ppanther, which again carries coiled tracks on the rear deck, note the dusty and faded condition of the paintwork on the vehicle.

Further evidence of Russian marksman ship, this time on Panther numbered 76. This close up picture shows details of the two brackets added to the gun mantlet to mount an optional searchlight unit.

2 x Max K. via Mirko Bayerl

One of the Panther ausf Gs in the line of abandoned tanks with the investigation number 75 showing the effects of the test firing of the Russian anti tank rounds. As with the subject model this Panther also carries coiled spare trak on the engine deck and shows details of the spare track hangers added to the turret sides by 23. Pz. Div. as a field modification to allow spare track to be hung on the turret to supliment the thinner turret side armour.

Max K. via Mirko Bayerl

by a Russian Sherman commander who came across the line of vehicles shortly after and he notes how the vehicles appeared in a uniform line, after the lead Russian tanks had fired on the line of tanks thinking these vehicles were combat capable, there was no response leading him to conclude they had been completely abandoned before his tanks had arrived.

After the first wave of Russians had passed the line of abandoned tanks, which included a Zwischenlosung that had been transferred to 23. Pz. Div. from 24. Pz. Div in January, the following Russian tanks used the vehicles for "target practice" (which was common practice). Members of a specialised Russian commission who were tasked with assessing German vehicles in turn followed these and how their tank rounds would perform against the German tanks armour and subsequently marking each vehicle with consecutive investigation numbers (Please see "The search for AJ9" by Mirko Bayerl for further information on this commission). I do not know what happened to the survivors of the abandoned vehicles some will have been captured and some will have perished in the maelstrom of the closing weeks of World War II on the Eastern front and perhaps some survived to make it to Germany and the safety of the American lines to surrender.

DML KIT 6370

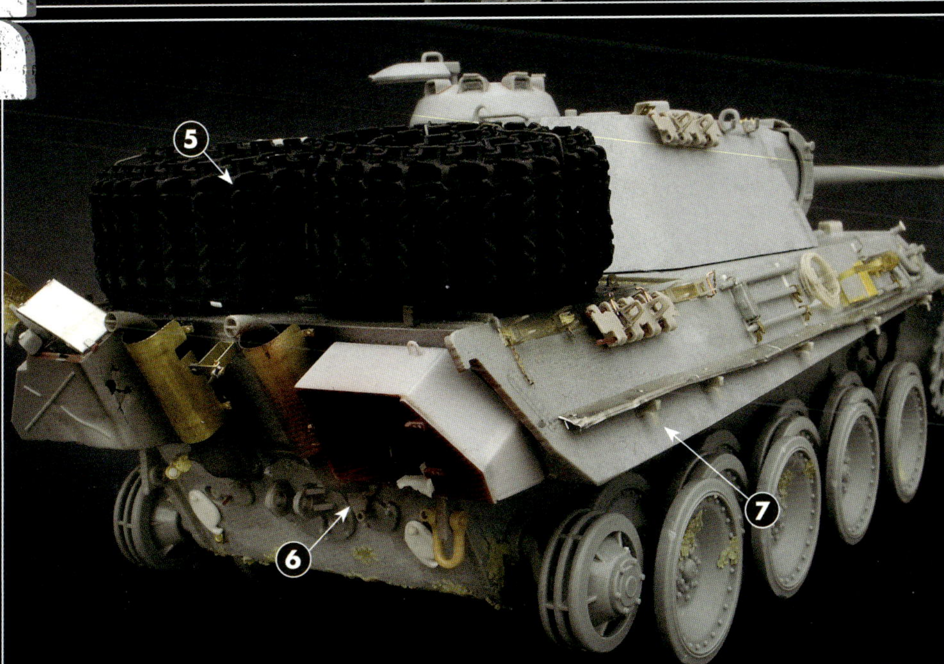

UPDATES OF THE KIT

1. Resin gun travel lock taken from the Accurate Armour Panther G update set as this part is better detailed than the kit part

2. Weld beads for the missing Schurtzen mounting bracket made from thin stretched sprue textured with a scapel and liquid cement.

3. Better detailed and more accurate WW2 productions resin track links are used for the spare tracks on the hull, with scratch built mounting brackets for the tracks used as extra armour on the turret sides.

4. The gun cleaning rod tube was fabricated from a length of styrene tube detailed with end caps supplied in the kit and Aber photo etch detail parts.

5. The "magic tracks" supplied in the kit were used for the coiled tracks on the engine deck to avoid having to go to the expense of a second set of WW2 productions tracks.

6. The open IR equipment stowage box is a casting taken from a master produced by Roddy MacDougall which he kindly supplied for this projectt.

7. The schurtzen rail was formed in sections from Pewter foil and fitted to the more accurate mounting brackets again supplied in the Accurate Armour update set. Frabricating the rails from pewter enabled me to easily repricate any battle damage.

Modelling "Mein Gott Ivan"

After studying the reference pictures, I had to hand and with help from Roddy MacDougall who pointed me in the correct direction with regard to details as to when the vehicle had been manufactured and what additions, I would need to make to correctly depict the vehicle I had chosen to model. We decided the best base kit for the project was Dragon models Steel Wheel Panther G kit 6370 as this includes all the relevant parts required to build a September/October production Panther, such as the correct cast armoured exhaust covers and a full set of rubber rimmed road wheels. I found no major issues with the construction of the kit, using a selection of after market accessories to enhance some of the kits details and reproduce the equipment and damage on the vehicle in my reference pictures, the main items being an Aber etch brass detail set, Accurate Armours resin panther update set and also WWII productions replacement resin tracks.

To enable me to depict battle damage on the schurtzen mounting rail I replaced the plastic kit components with new rails fabricated from pewter foil sheet. The open IR stowage box was kindly donated to me by Roddy, this was a resin casting of a master Roddy had made of which a limited number cast by M.A. Mori. To depict the extra load carrying the coiled track on the engine deck I decided to lower the rear suspension by removing the location pins on the suspension arms and positioning them at a lower angle to give a "tail heavy" look, also during the construction I decided to add the coils of spare track to the engine deck, as fitting them after the vehicle had been painted may have lead to potential problems of getting the track to sit correctly without damaging the paintwork. To avoid the expense of a second set of WWII production tracks I opted to use the kit supplied "magic tracks" which although not as well detailed as the resin offerings still look good and would be more than acceptable to depict the coiled tracks on the engine deck.

With the main construction finished I added some "mud deposits" to the lower hull

An overall view of the completed model showing the interation between the crew members as they notice the advancing Russian vehicles in the distance.

and road wheels using epoxy putty , trying to replicate the areas of dried mud as shown in the reference photograph I was working to. After checking for any obvious omissions or faults, I began the painting stage.

From the start of the painting, I had in my mind that I wanted to try to depict a vehicle with a faded and dusty appearance that had been the result of hard fighting in the harsh Hungarian environmentighting in the harsh Hungarian environment.

Painting began with the model receiving an overall coat of a dark Black /Brown mix made up from Humbrol matt Black and matt Chocolate enamel colours; this was applied via my airbrush in two well-thinned coats paying particular attention to ensure this colour mix covered all of the bare plastic. The reason behind using the Black/brown mix was both at act as a primer for the different materials on the model and to act as a pre shading coat that would help to give depth and create shadows in the following paint applications. With the model under coated the first of the three tone camouflage colours are added using my airbrush , first came the dark yellow base colour mixed from Humbrol enamels numbers 94+81 and 74 this gave me a very light paint tone. I always start from light colours with rather vibrant tones as I have found a lighter colour can be darkened down but it is very difficult to lighten a dark colour efficiently, once this first coat had dried to further enhance the colour tones I further lightened the paint mix by adding a small amount of matt White and proceeded carefully airbrush this mix onto the hulls upper surfaces and turret top, taking care to have a gradual lightening of the base yellow.

Leaving the yellow to dry for 24 hours, I then cut masks for the camouflage pattern following closely the factory applied "Daimler Benz pattern" and after the masks had been applied to the model airbrushing the camouflage pattern could begin. The Green colour was mixed again from Humbrol colours using colour number 225 lightened with a small amount of 120 and once this had been applied I removed some portions of the mask and sprayed the

PANTHER AUSF.G

Red Brown sections of the pattern using a base colour of Humbrol 133 lightened with some 153 (as a note about the colours and colour mixes I have used, I tend to mix the colours by eye so it is difficult to give exact mixing ratios, also I realise the colours tones will change as a result of the subsequent weathering processes).

Once the masking had been fully removed I was left with quite a garish looking model with very bright colours, the next step was to introduce some harmony to the colours to try and get them to sit together on the model. I have found the best way to achieve this is to carefully dry brush each of the individual colours using the same basic mixes as applied with the airbrush but this time mixing in a small amount of Humbrol flesh tone into the colours, then using a small flat brush and a gentle scrubbing motion gradually work over each of the individual colour patches until you achieve what can best be described as a general fading of the camouflage colours. The key to carrying out this successfully is to take your time doing only small areas at a time and gradually building up the amount of Flesh tone in the mix.

Now the Panther looked a lot more harmonised but still very bright. Subsequent layers of "filter" washes(these are layers of heavily thinned paint floated over the main panels of the model but not allowed to collect around any of the detail like a pin wash, these filters gradually darken down the paint tones and further harmonises the camouflage colours) mixed up from various browns and reds in the Humbrol range.

Now happy with the general tones of the model the national and unit markings were added using rub down decals from the excellent Archer transfers range, following there application I sealed in the paintwork and decals with a Polyurethane satin varnish applied via my airbrush, which once dried protected the underlying paint from the further weathering procedures. It was now time to add some depth to the details with controlled pin washes of burnt umber oil paints, by which the heavily thinned oil paint was touched onto detailed parts such as weld seams and tool clamps then capillary action would cause the paint to naturally flow around the detail adding a

This front 3/4 view shows the layers of damage and dirt which has built up over a period of combat in the harsh conditions of the war on the Eastern front.

subtle shadow. The process of pin washing various parts followed by adding delicate highlights carried on for a number of days, being careful not to over exaggerate either the washes or highlights trying to keep a balance at all times. To further impart the sense of a vehicle which had seen a lot of action, I started to add a number of paint chips and scratches to strategic areas on the model where paint would natural wear and scuff away on the real vehicle such as around hatches, the engine deck and where the crew would mount and dismount the vehicle. Large areas of chipping were replicated by dabbing a dark brown paint mix onto the required areas using a small piece of dense foam which(such as comes with packaging of electrical goods) gives a very effective representation of damaged and chipped paint, these patches were further refined with small scratches painted in using a fine brush. Again, all of the scuffs and chips were deliberately underplayed to keep a balance to the paintwork.

Next, the remaining tools, insides of the open hatches, exhaust pipes and other details were painted in using both enamel and acrylic paints (using whichever medium was best suited for the task). As all of these other items were painted they were carefully weathered using the same methods as the rest of the model so no one item would look out of place, the spare tracks on the turret side received some extra attention by undercoating them in a dark yellow base coat then extensively sponging a dark brown /steel grey mix over the yellow followed by burnt Umber oil washes to give the impression they were spare track had taken from another vehicle and at one stage in their life had been over painted in the same base colour as the vehicle they came from.

With the majority of the painting on the turret and upper hull complete my attention turned to the mud and dust deposits on the lower hull, I began by painting in the mud deposits I had added at the construction stage, these were blocked in using a dark brown mix made up from equal amounts of Humbrol 110 and 155 and once these had fully cured further heavy washes of enamels made up from various combinations mixed by eye of Humbrol 33/ 98 /110/155 were floated on to the lower hull blending from

23. PZ. DIVISION

dark to light tones. At one time I would have been very close to calling this model now finished, but after further studies of my reference photographs and conversations with Mirko about the conditions the fighting forces in Hungary had to suffer I felt the model still lacked a sense of "feeling" it did not yet have the impression that I had in my mind it would look like when I started the project. After a lot of deliberation I felt that the model still looked too clean and clinical, it was lacking layers of dust and dirt that would have accumulated during its life, to represent this I mix up a heavily thinned amount of Humbrol Matt 72 which is a excellent colour for dried on dirt and grime. The mix was carefully applied to areas on the turret and hull (again taking care to place the mix in logical places where dust would gather) then with a large brush moistened with thinners the dust mix was carefully blended into the paintwork, with almost a stabbing motion on the turret and hull upper faces and streaked in a downward motion on the turret and hull sides leaving traces of dust accumulated around detail and the areas that would act as a natural trap. After reworking these areas two or three times I adding and blending more of the matt 72 I felt now the model reflected more closely the look and Feeling I wished to portray. Throughout the painting a weathering processes described above I had deliberately not included the coiled tracks on the engine deck as they had only recently been placed there they would not show the same amount of weathering, they were painted to show much more surface rust as if they had been stored in the repair depot waiting to be fitted to a vehicle. These tracks were base coated in a mix again from Humbrol enamels of numbers 111,186and 98 which was then treated to various blue grey and rust tones washes, with the track outer surfaces finally being lightly dry brushed with Vallejo German camouflage black green acrylic to bring out some of the track patterns details.

Figures, bringing the model to life

One of the main elements in this story I knew from the beginning would be the figures and their individual interactions, I wanted to give the figures a look of worry and surprise

by what appears to be approaching Russians in the distance. With this in mind, I quickly realised that it would be very difficult to find stock figures, which would fit my needs so I decided that the only way to get the correct feeling and look would be to adapt and convert existing figures.

The first thing was to find a set of figures that had roughly the uniform and proportions I needed, one set that really stood out was the Dragon models "Achtung Jabo" set as I felt the poses of the figures would not need too much alteration and the working denim uniform of the figures would fit my needs perfectly. I had an estimate of how I wanted the interaction between the figures to workout with one of the crewmembers alerting the other crewmember as to the coming danger whilst they were enjoying a short rest bite from their frantic retreat.

Combining different parts from the Dragon set I managed to roughly pose and position the figures, quite a lot of additional work was required in the form of scratch building some of the figures arms and items of clothing such as the winter trousers on the figure on the engine deck and the open jacket of the pointing figure, all of these items were built using Magic sculpt epoxy putty.

To give me the required facial attitudes I replaced the figures heads with items from the Hornet and Alpine ranges trying to find faces that best expressed the feelings I was trying to convey, with the main bodies and uniforms of the figures fleshed out so to speak I proceeded to further enhanced the uniform details using etch brass insignia and badges.

The figures where then primed using an acrylic primer applied via an aerosol can and further checked for an imperfections that may require attention before the main painting could commence. All of the painting of the figures was carried out using acrylic paint using a method of building up very thin layers of highlights over a base coat, the uniforms were deliberately painted in slightly different tones on each figure to try and give each figure a degree of individuality, also the tones of the flesh and uniform colours were kept subdued with a degree of dirt added to the clothing in an effort to enhance the look of well used clothing and the crews exhaustion. The

figure in the turret hatch was given a deep red pullover to give the impression that by this late stage in the conflict the supply situation was such that the crews had to use civilian clothing to replace worn out regulation uniforms, this also had the advantage of providing a focal point for the figure group. Once the painting of all of the figures had been completed, they were attached to the Panther using epoxy glue taking care to keep the figures in the correct positions.

Base and Groundwork

Looking at my reference photos I wanted to try to portray the unfinished road surface and part of the ditch on the side of the road, as a base just depicting the flat road surface would look lifeless and not give the vignette a great sense of height. With these thoughts in my mind I opted to build an elevated base which would enable me to include the ditch section, the main body of the base was built up using two blocks of insulation board which is very light and easy to carve and form. After gluing the sections on top of each other, I squared the edges off to get the correct size I required, then carved away the ditch section using a variety of files and knifes until I had something in the rough shape of the ditch. The edges of the base were then blanked off using plastic card cut to the profile of the insulation board, the edges then being filled and sanded to hide any unsightly join marks, and then the sides were painted in satin black using an automotive spray can. The material to make up the dolomite of the road surface was not a problem as on one of his last research trips to Hungary Mirko had collected a number of stones from the actual ditch at the site of the road on which the Panther was abandoned, Mirko kindly passed these stones onto me for this project.

The stones were carefully crushed down to smaller in scale particles ready to be added to the base, once I had enough of the crushed stone to easily cover the base, I mixed up some household filler which was coloured using sand and light brown acrylic paint (by colouring the filler it meant I would not have to repaint the base to get rid of any unsightly white areas of filler).

The filler was then carefully spread out

This close up shows the figures worn uniforms, also the different weathering effects appiled to the turret mounted spare tracks and the coiled tracks on the engine deck.

over the base foam, levelling it out on the road surface and building up the features in the section of ditch. With the filler still wet, the crushed stone was arranged over the filler and worked into the wet filler with a damp paintbrush until I was happy with how the stone sat in the filler. After shaking, the excess stones off I set the whole base aside to dry for 24 hours. Returning to the base after the drying time elapsed the plaster had dried to a pleasing light tan colour that acted well with the natural colouration of the stones, to add a little depth to the groundwork various washes of brown and sand enamel paints were applied to give some variation and tone to the groundwork. To add some further interest to the base I added an abandoned oil drum in the bottom of the ditch, which had been painted and weathered with acrylic paints before being glued in place.

With the oil drum in place all that was left was to secure the foam board to a wooden base and fix the panther to the base carefully blending the vehicle into the groundwork using small amounts of dust coloured modelling pigment powders.

Acknowledgements

Firstly and foremost I would like to thank Mirko Bayerl for his outstanding contribution in supplying the then and now photographs and a history behind the vehicle I had chosen to depict in model form, also for his limitless patience in dealing with all of the requests for information I made of him through out the building of the model. Roddy MacDougall for supplying the IR box and keeping me pointed in the right direction concerning the production differences required to reproduce the Panther in the picture. In addition, my parents for many years ago buying me my first armour kit and sacrificing many a Friday night to take me to my local model club meetings.

Thank you all!

Lester Plaskitt

A head on view of the of the completed model on its road way diorama base.

THE LAST OF THE

I./Pz.Regt. 22, April,1945

STEEL WHEELERS

Darren Gawle had to tackle a sudden turn of events with his Steel Wheel Panther, as it turned out the vehicle he modelled actually belonged to a different unit than was originally thought.

One of the most attractive things about modelling late-war German armour is that some 65 years after the end of the War, there are still plenty of new photographs emerging which re-define what we know about the Panzerwaffe. Unfortunately, in the frequent absence of what might be termed a 'smoking gun' regarding unit identification, we resort to theory and educated guesswork. Not infrequently, the results can be very frustrating indeed.

Background

This project began when, in comparing photo references with a colleague, it was brought to my attention that photos of two different steel-wheeled (or 'SW') Panthers shared similar unit-level modifications. Two of the photos can be found in either Wydawnictwo Publishing's Panzerwaffe 1945 series or in Frontline Illustration's similar German Larger Panzer Units series; they are of a knocked-out SW Panther with the fgst.nr. '121039'. Another pair of photos came to me via a private collector and show another (abandoned) SW Panther, this time with a turret number visible: '424'. Equally as interesting, this Panther also features a rubber-rimmed roadwheel assembly at one station.

I had originally intended to build a model of '424' even before I'd heard about this book project, but once the unit connection was made between '121039' and '424' I developed a deeper interest in finding out which unit it was who'd received a shipment of at least two SW Panthers and performed some interesting modifications to their tool stowage. Firstly, on both vehicles, the brackets for the tool stowage have been cut off (either with a grinding wheel or a blowtorch; I can't tell given the resolution of the photos) except for the towing cable lugs at the front of each hull side. Further, the stowage tubes have been relocated to the engine decks; also, on '121039' at least, hangers for spare tracks have been added to the rear turret sides.

None of the photos feature any useful landmarks, but with a little observation some hints can be gathered - '121039' was photographed by Soviet cameramen, so it would follow that it was lost on the eastern front; and while there are some unidentifiable houses in the photos of '424', they feature brickwork which is a dead ringer for the style found in East Prussia – or at least, that was what I thought originally!

After cross-referencing deliveries of Panthers during a timeframe in which some of them might have been steel-wheelers with units which fought on the Eastern Front, and exchanging e-mails with Martin Block and Ian Michael Wood, I arrived at the opinion that these two tanks most likely belonged to I./Fallschirm-Panzer Regiment 'Hermann Goering' with a lesser chance that they belonged to I./Pz.Rgt. 31 of 5 Panzer Division.

And so, proceeding along this tack I finished my model as a Hermann Goering vehicle only to see, a full month after sending all my photos and text for this article in, a new photo of '424' emerged, showing sightseeing American GIs posing on the wreck. Back to the drawing board...

US forces did not end the war in East Prussia, so Hermann Goering was out as a possible unit. After consulting with some European contacts, it was established that the location of the photo could probably be Oberhoffen, in Alsace, so now it looked like the unit could be I./Pz.Rgt. 22 of 21 Panzer Division. Certainly 21 Pz.Div. ended the war fighting the Red Army in the vicinity of Cottbus, which would explain photos of another vehicle of the same unit in Russian

UPDATES OF THE KIT

1. MA Morii resin cupola. Resin details from Accurate Armour were also used.
2. PE screens from the kit, other PE details from Aber
3. Weld beads from thin plastic sprue.
4. Schürzen rails made from scratch using copper sheet.
5. Armour plate textured using stippled Gunze Mr. Surfacer which was then sanded.
6. WW2 Productions spare tracks.
7. Stowage tube scratchbuilt using copper sheet and Aber PE.

DML KIT 6370

archives. Interestingly, it would appear that 21 Pz.Div. acquired its SW Panthers when it inherited vehicles from the disbanded 112 Panzer Brigade in October 1944. Certainly, 21 Pz.Div. did not acquire any factory-fresh Panthers during that window of opportunity in September and October 1944 when 1 SS-Pz.Div. 'LSSAH' and I./Pz.Rgt. 24 (two units known to have operated SW Panthers in the west) acquired theirs. It remains unclear exactly where 112 Pz.Brig. would have got SW Panthers from - but I./Pz.Rgt. 130 did draw new Panthers during this September-October 1944 timeframe, and as 112 Pz.Brig. did inherit Panthers from I./Pz.Rgt. 130 before itself being disbanded and passing its remaining vehicles on to Pz.Rgt. 22, then Panzer Lehr appears the likely source.

The model

I naturally chose the DML SW Panther kit (#6370) for this project; while it suffers from a modest number of minor faults, it's still a better choice than the still-available Tamiya SW Panther kit in terms of detail and dimensions. Enough has been written about this kit elsewhere, so as far as this article is concerned, I'm only concentrating on details relevant to this build.

After consulting what very few photos I've got of Panthers whose tool brackets have come adrift, I came up with my best guess as to the locations of the spot welds which held the brackets to the hull; these I simulated with stretched sprue textured with a hot knife, while retaining the relevant tow cable lugs

Scratch built stowage boxes from copper and Moskit exhausts were also added.

and supports where they should have been had they still been part of the tool brackets. The relocated stowage tube was scratchbuilt from copper sheet to allow it to dent more realistically - I could find no reference which shows clearly how the tow cable U-brackets on the engine deck were relocated (n.b. they would have had to have been in order for the stowage tube to fit properly) so after a photo in the frontispiece of Germany's Panther Tank, I simply left them off. The stowage bins I also elected to partially rebuild with copper sheet for denting purposes, as can be seen in the pre-paint photos.

On the right-hand side hull front, I replaced one of the tow cable lugs with a hook as used for the turret track stowage; one of the photos of '121039' shows this detail and may have as likely been a unit modification as it may have been a field-expedient repair. I used the kit-supplied track-hanging hooks for the turret track stowage as well - again, no clear views are available of how the unit did this, so I elected to cut off the horizontal reinforcing bar on each of the hangers as the ones in the kit are, in appearance, specific to 'LSSAH'.

By the time construction was well underway, I had decided that I was going to build neither '424' nor '121039', but rather an 'unphotographed' SW Panther of I./Fallschirm-Panzer Regiment 'Hermann Goering' (as I was still working under the theory that 'HG' was the unit) so that I could exercise a little creativity and creative license within the boundaries I'd set for myself. To this end I chose the turret number '321' and, based on the info in Panzer Tracts, the fgst.nr. '121045'.

Before painting, I spent some time looking at available photos of SW Panthers where the camouflage patterns are visible. In a pinch, the kind of camouflage scheme applied by the assembly firm M.A.N. in the early autumn of 1944 would be accurate, but there are a number of unique little details to

The weld seams are very prominent on the finished model, giving a realistic impression.

Note the "liberated" civilian shackle used to secure the end of the tow cable and the stains in the dirt and dust on the engine deck.

The tracks were partially painted white and carefully masked off with home made masks to create the numbers.

the schemes applied to SW Panthers which make them unique - as though the paint shop at M.A.N. hadn't yet settled on the 'classic' scheme which would be applied to most of the Panthers from October onwards. '121039' does appear to feature a somewhat indistinct version of the 'classic' M.A.N. scheme; however, '424' appears to be so coated in winter whitewash that hardly any scheme is visible at all. I decided I wanted to try a variation on the scheme sported by the factory-fresh fgst.nr. '121052' of which there are three excellent views in Panzer Tracts 5-3, with allowances made for my own personal tastes and creative urges. Before the camouflage pattern was sprayed, though, I applied a primer red colour to areas where the stowage brackets would have been, and masked these off.

As far as the paint mixes themselves, I have to admit that I'm not a purist when it comes to brands or even enamels vs. acrylics. I use whatever I feel gives me the colours, tones, or shades I'm looking for. I almost never use colours straight from the bottle or tin, either. Through trial and error, I've settled on a 50-50 mix of Humbrol numbers 72 and 83 lightened with white for my dunkelgelb (a similar mix using Gunze 336 Hemp and 71 Middle Stone can also be achieved if acrylics are your thing) I preferred Tamiya acrylics (XF-10 Brown cut with a little XF-9 Hull Red and darkened with a little black) for the rottbraun in this build, while the green was a mix of Tamiya XF-26 Deep Green and Gunze 312 lightened with Tamiya XF-21 Sky. All markings bar the numbers on the track links are Archer dry transfers. The white numbers on the turret track stowage were reverse-masked; i.e., the tracks, after priming in black were spot-painted white where the numbers would go. After I masked the

Pastels and pigments was used to carry earth tones up the lower part of the standing figure's trousers.

numbers by cutting the relevant numbers out of masking tape, I continued to paint the tracks as normal, removing the number masks when the paint had dried.

Regarding weathering, again I had to take a couple of days to decide on a course of action – this also was due to my original plan to build an 'HG' Panther and set it towards the end of November 1944. I think that this is the only area where the turn of events regarding the change of unit to I./ Pz.Rgt. 22 worked in my favour, as now I could set the model later in 1945 when it would have had a chance to sustain more damage and weathering. In truth, I probably originally weathered it a bit too much for a vehicle in service for only a couple of months. But while I feel that detractors of the 'chipping' style of weathering have a point which is unfortunately underscored by modellers who go overboard with this technique, at the same time the detractors invariably fail to account for the effects hobnail boots, shrapnel, forest growth, and debris sent flying by artillery bursts would have on a tank's finish in even a short period of time.

The figures

I lept at the chance to use Alpine Miniatures' 'German Heer Panzer Crew #1' figure (#35084) because it represents a crewman wearing a leather Luftwaffe one-piece bomber suit; this was entirely accurate for Fallschirm-Panzer Division 'Hermann Goring', as I'd originally intended. Luckily, these suits were also not unusual amongst Heer crewmen, and as I had originally painted the figure with a Luftwaffe blue sidecap all I needed to do was re-paint his headgear and swap the Luftwaffe cap and uniform patches for Heer examples to effect the final correction. I also chose the commander figure from Tank's 'German SS tank crew, Summer 1940-45' set (#35005)

The spare track links were painted separately in different shades of browns and then re-assembled them randomly for tonal variation.

but swapped the kit's head for a spare Alpine head and made some cosmetic changes to his uniform. Uniform patches were, like the Panther's markings, from Archer, although in this case the patches are so small and difficult (well, for me anyway) to apply in the usual method that I ended up applying them to clear decal film and affixing then to the figures as wet transfers.

Acknowledgements

In addition to thanking the editor for the opportunity to participate in this project, and the team in general for the ongoing encouragement, this article would not have happened without the technical input and feedback of Roddy MacDougall, Mirko Bayerl, and Manus Gallagher. Thanks also go out to Martin Block, Ian Michael Wood, and Paul Ranta for their gracious assistance during the original writing of this article when I still thought that 'HG' was the unit; with this group I would also like to extend special thanks to Lee Archer, Hans Weber, Timm Haasler, and Fred Déprun for sharing the new information regarding 21 Pz. Div. with me in time to make the necessary corrections.

Happily, the new photo of '424' should be included in a future volume of Lee Archer and William Auerbach's Panzerwrecks series.

Darren Gawle

Bibliography

de Meyer, Haasler, MacDougall, Vosters & Weber (2007) Duel In The Mist: The Leibstandarte During The Ardennes Offensive vol.1 (ISBN 978-0-9555413-0-8)

Duffy, Christopher (1991) Red Storm On The Reich: The Soviet March On Germany, 1945 (ISBN 0-415-03589-9)

Jentz, Thomas L. & Doyle, Hilary Louis (2004) Panzer Tracts No.5-3: Panzerkampfwagen "Panther" Ausfuhrung G (ISBN 0-9744862-7-2)

Jentz, Thomas L. & Doyle, Hilary Louis (1995) Germany's Panther Tank: The Quest For Combat Supremacy (ISBN 0-88740-812-5)

Kolomyjec, Maksym & Moszczanskij, Ilja (2004) Wydawnictwo Militaria 198: Panzerwaffe 1945, vol.1 (ISBN 83-7219-184-0)

Perrigault, Jean-Claude (2003) 21 Panzer Division (ISBN 978-2840481577)

Urbanke, Axel (2009) Endkampf um das Reichsgebeit 1944-1945 (ISBN 978-3-941437-02-9)

Kortenhaus, Werner (2007) 21. Panzerdivision 1943-1945 (ISBN 978-3935107112)

THE LAST OF THE STEEL WHEELERS

Mirko Bayerl presents a comprehensive article about Panther AJ9. This particular vehicle had for years intrigued many people, and after careful investigation he finally identified not only the vehicle's unit but the actual location where it was eventually destroyed by its crew.

Part 1: the search for AJ9,
Part 2: history of AJ9 and 9.SS.Pz.Div. Hohenstaufen in Hungary
Part 3: construction of the diorama with Panther AJ9

PART 1: THE SEARCH FOR AJ9

Max K. via Mirko Bayerl

Ever since the Russian book "Boi u ozera Balaton" or "The battle of Lake Balaton" by Max Kolomiets was published in 1999 have I been fascinated by the immense waste of material that took place in Hungary in March 1945. The Germans abandoned and blew up a tremendous amount of tanks and other vehicles during the latter part of March. The reason for this was of course the rapid Russian advance, which aimed to reach Austria and Vienna as quickly as possible. This together with lack of fuel, ammunition, and the risk of ending up in Russian captivity were also important factors in these losses. Operational tanks were in some cases left intact, though the crews always tried to destroy them if possible. Some divisions were forced to leave what was almost their entire compliment of tanks and other vehicles in a very short time period before retreating westwards. Those that still had fuel were often forced out on the fields due to the traffic jams caused by the retreating forces and refugees. These often ended up bogged down on their bellies in the marshy fields. Very few of these tanks could be recovered due both to a lack of time and fuel and that Werkstatt units were also forced to blow up and abandon their vehicles.

For the past ten years, I have been fascinated by the tanks in the Balaton book, wondering about the story surrounding every one of them. It is hard to find definite answers to most of these questions since many Russian sources and diaries promote "victories" describing many knocked out vehicles even if the truth about the vehicles is more often as described earlier. The fact is, that the Russians in many cases shot at vehicles that were already abandoned and then credited them as victories. Each of the German wrecks was later registered and examined by Russian evaluation teams. They were also numbered by special teams from the Artillery

Headquarters of the 3rd Ukrainian Front, the 17th Air Army in co-operation with other departments and commissions from the Russian army. Altogether, 968 knocked out, abandoned and destroyed vehicles were registered, including approximately 450 armoured troop carriers of different models. About 400 of the vehicles were marked with a white, lime based paint and were documented as to how they had been destroyed. If any dead crew members were found, this was also recorded. For some reason many of the vehicles registered in February 1945 were again registered in April/March 1945. A similar registration system is said to have been used after the Kursk battle in 1943.

Identifying what units the tanks in the Balaton area belonged to is almost impossible. Many photos are poor quality and most vehicles are covered a layer of dirt, mud, and soot which makes any tactical and divisional markings difficult to see.

Some of the vehicles in the book caught my interest more than others, in particular a Befehlspanther with an unusual and intriguing turret number AJ9. My first thoughts were that it could probably have belonged to any of the Waffen SS divisions that operated in Hungary in 1945. However, what did AJ9 stand for? The topic was frequently discussed on internet forums on and off for years and many ideas and different theories were proposed. Could AJ9 have stood for an Artillery observation vehicle? Many Divisions were suggested as the potential parent. I was fascinated by this mystery and tried every channel of information I could think of, including advertising in a veteran's magazine in Germany, hoping to get some answers. The lack of response only created more questions; was AJ9 knocked out or blown up by its crew, who commanded it, where was it photographed?

If I could find the location were AJ9 was left, maybe it would be easier to identify the unit to that it had belonged, but the house in the background of the photo is a typical Hungarian house which can be found anywhere in Hungary. The only thing I knew for sure was that the photo was taken somewhere near Lake Balaton.

Possible break through?

While I continued to discuss AJ9 and other "mysterious" Panthers with their cryptic turret numbers it was time for methodical research. One of the pictures previously mentioned in discussions had been taken by Kriegsberichter Rottensteiner and shows a Waffen-SS Panther with the turret number 99 in the Ardennes, another picture taken in the Czech territories in May 1945 also shows a Panther with the turret number 99. Now things were getting hot. Did Panther 99 and AJ9 have anything in common and were they possibly from the same unit? Both were Befehlspanthers and were produced at roughly the same time in October 1944. Parts of the Stab of SS.Pz.Rgt 2 were located further north in Czechoslovakia at the end of April 1945. They were also in the Ardennes in December and January 1944-45. Now I was almost certain that AJ9 belonged to part of the Stab of Das Reich. I travelled to Hungary to visit the battlefields where the division operated in March 1945 during the Spring Awakening offensive, hoping to possibly find the location I was looking for. One of the areas I went to was the remains of the mansion called Heinrich Major near Sárkeresztúr, where heavy fighting had taken place in March 1945. The mansion area was quickly given the name "Alcázar" by the German defenders, after a famous Spanish fortress (Toledo) that had been legendary for the Nationalists, which they defended against the Republicans during the Spanish civil war. At this point, I was almost certain that AJ 9 had been operating in this area, which inspired me to start modelling this vehicle in 1/35.

So, could AJ9's final resting place be found here? I decided to follow the route that 2.SS Pz.Div. Das Reich took after the fighting ceased and they were ordered to go to another combat area. Heinrich Major was abandoned after both sides had suffered heavy casualties in men and material.

All the tanks and material from the 2.SS. Pz.Div marched to Herend, where they were loaded on to railway cars and went to the area around Komarom and Kisber in order to prevent a total breakthrough by Russian forces there. The transport took place at night between the 19-20 March. There was no fighting during their transport up to Herend and we did not find any buildings like those in the AJ 9 photo in Sárkeresztúr. I concluded that AJ 9 might be somewhere else altogether that it would be difficult and tricky to find. I was not so familiar with the area...I was about to give up... time was running out as well as my motivation... somehow I decided to go on and I decided not to give up.

Two photographs showing a Befehlspanther, one from the Ardennes with the tactical number 99 which I first suspected belonged to SS.Pz.Rgt 9 Hohenstaufen. However, it was later confirmed that it to belonged to SS.Pz.Rgt 2 Das Reich and was most likely used by the commander of the I.Abt.SS.Pz.Rgt 2, SS Hstuf Willi Matzke. The inset photo shows a Befehlspanther with the tactical numbers 99 I 02 after it was left in a vehicle dump at Znojmo (Znaim) in Czechoslovakia. It is almost certain that this vehicle belongs to SS.Pz. Rgt 2 as well. The addition of the digits I 02 can be explained by it having been taken over by the adjutant, Ustuf R. Reichenbacher, in the last few months of the war. This Befehlspanther is probably the same vehicle as the one photographed in the Ardennes with the tactical number 99. In the latter stages of the war, SS. Pz.Rgt 2 used tactical numbers containing a "9" on their stabs and company vehicles, i.e. R99, 99, 98, 299, 298. During the Normandy campaign, a similar numbering system was used. The Stab of the regiment used 99 (Tychsen), 98 (Rupp) and 97 (Kuhlmann). The 9.SS.Hohenstaufen which was also part of II SS Pzr. Korps used the numbers KO9, AJ9 and 009 on their vehicles.

AMC and Milos collection

The real break through

During my trips to Hungary I have met many historians and enthusiasts who share the same interest as me; the fighting in Hungary in 1945. I have undertaken numerous trips through the years, visiting battlefields, documenting and collecting as much information as I could. I had also become good friends with many Hungarians who followed me on my trips to the Hungarian countryside with great enthusiasm.

I learned that there was an enthusiast, who like me, had tried to indentify vehicles from the Balaton-book and had tried to indentify the places where the vehicles were photographed, enabling "then and now" comparisons. I was pleasantly surprised to hear that he had already found the Tiger II with the tactical number 123 (Russian reg. number 101) from S.Pz.Abt. 509, the Jagd.Pz. IV 70 (V) with tactical number 333 (Russian reg. number 104) and the Jagdpanther, with the evaluation number 102 as well as having the tactical number 102. Both of theses vehicles were from S.Pz.Jg.Abt 560. All were located near the town of Balatonfüzfö, which today is a

A dump near the railway station in Balatonfüzfö, at Lake Balaton's north eastern corner. The picture shows Russian and German vehicles awaiting transport to Hungarian and Russian facilities where they will be scrapped and melted down. The hull from AJ9 can probably be seen half way up the road. It can be identified by the bent turret ring, the missing gun cleaning tools tube, the brackets for the towing clevis as well as other small details. The village of Vilonya is near by and AJ 9 was towed to Balatonföző, as were the other vehicles in the picture, so they were not knocked out here. We can also see a Marder III Ausf. M from 1.Pz.Div. (9/Pz.Gren.Rgt 1 or AA-1) which listed two of these vehicles in its inventory or 23.Pz.Div. (stab Pz.Jg.Abt 128) which lists one in mid March 1945. Two Panthers from 1.SS.Pz.Div. LAH can also be seen with the turret numbers 212 and 222. They were probably left behind after the division's transport to Varpalota between Lepsény and Berhida. We can see a Jagdpanther from s.Pz.Jg.Abt 560, a StuG III from Sturm.Art.Brig 303 (3202, this unit had 4 digit tactical numbers) and a Wirbelwind from either s.Pz.Abt 509 or 1.SS. A further Jagdpanther, Pz.IV, Hetzer and a number of T-34's can also be seen at this collection point. It is not certain when this picture was taken. It could be from March/April 1945 but is more likely to be a year later. An eyewitness claims that AJ9 stood in Vilonya for a year before it was towed away, and it is unlikely that resources would be used to transport the wrecks immediately after the battle.

Novosti

vibrant tourist site just by the shore of Lake Balaton's north east corner. I also had the opportunity to see a photograph from this area, which I was told was taken in March or April 1945. In this photo a large number of German and Russian wrecks have been collected near the railway station to be sent for scrap. My mind started working... We had identified the location of Russian evaluation numbers 99 to 103 in this area. AJ9 has the evaluation number 111, did this mean that the wreck site of AJ9 was also to be found nearby, could it be that simple? We knew that the evaluation number order was not always chronological and did not always made sense, but we felt that we were slowly finding a "key" to identifying the locations we were looking for and actually found that in several cases the vehicles stood close to each other and were numbered consecutively. We took a closer look at the photo from Balatofüzfö and discovered a Panther with similar damage to AJ9, could this be AJ9?

However, if AJ9 was operating in this area it could not have belonged to 2.SS Pz.Div as they were stationed much further north. So, what number was closest to 111? There was a Hummel marked 113 and a StuG III marked as 116. At this point, we had not yet identified the location of 112 which we will come back to later on. We concluded that number 116 had belonged to 23. Pz.Div, and was stuck in mud and abandoned at Mano Major, which we had already identified and the Hummel 113 seemed to be standing by

Balatonfüzfö today. The railway line and the surrounding landscape made the comparison with the photo from 1945/46 to the left fairly easy.

This late version Hummel was knocked out or blown up in Peremarton during the battle in mid March 1945. It probably belonged to SS. Pz. Art. Rgt.9. Note the characteristic brick wall in the background, enabling a positive identification of the area. The Hummel has the Russian evaluation team number 113. This particular vehicle would later prove to be the key element in the search for AJ9.

Max K. via Mirko Bayerl

the side of a main road. Maybe it wouldn't be too hard to find the location? We were closing in on AJ9. Unfortunately I could not continue the search on this trip as I had to return to Sweden, but a new trip was planned. We went back to Balatonfüzfö in November 2008, bringing photos and maps. We asked elderly locals for any clue they could give. Some of them believed that Berhida was the town we were looking for, so off we went. We met with an historian who told us that there had not been any knocked out or abandoned German vehicles in Berhida in March 1945, just a few Russian tanks. This very helpful man would later play an important role is finding the location of AJ9. We went back to Balatonfüzfö and met with another historian who claimed he recognised the house in the background of the photo of AJ9. Bingo! We set off to find the spot and once there we were convinced we were in the right place in Balatonfüzfö, we jumped with joy! We met an old lady who had lived in the house and she also confirmed it was the right place and she also told us that there had been a German wreck sitting outside their house in March 1945.

Our euphoria was short lived however. An old man who also lived nearby was called in and took a look at the picture, he said the house was not the one in the picture and that the vehicle in front of the house had not been a tank but a light troop carrier. We took a closer look and soon realised there were details on the houses and other items in the picture that did not match. Our spirits were very low having spent a lot of time there convinced we had found AJ9's location. We went back to Budapest, we had run out of time for now and it was getting dark, the mood travelling back in the car was even darker!

When summing up our trip, we remembered what the local historian in Balatonfüzfö had said. He recognised the fence in the background of the photo showing Hummel 113 in Peremarton. He had been wrong about AJ9 but sounded very confident that 113 stood in Peremarton. His information and Hummel 113 would later prove to be the key to solving the mystery with AJ9. Peremarton is an industrial area in the town of Berhida and heavy fighting took place here between 20-22 March. The 9. SS Pz.Div Hohenstaufen was in the middle of this battle.

It was time for me to return to Sweden for now, but the team and I kept in touch, discussing the possible location of AJ9 and in which villages we might find the location in the future. We knew that somehow, somewhere, we would find it if we just spent enough time searching for it. I kept studying diaries, divisional reports, maps, photos and other documents and this investigation

This picture shows SS-Ostuf. Bauer who was the Adjutant to the Regiment commander, Otto Meyer. The picture was taken in April 1944. Note the turret number AJ9.

Another picture of AJ9 from 9.SS.Pz.Div Hohenstaufen at Tarnopol, April 1944. The Pz. IV in the background could be the signals' officer's vehicle, with the turret number 009.

turned into a detective's work.

So what units had been in this area in March 1945? 1. SS Pz. Div. LAH was up north at Varpalota/Litér, and 9. SS Pz. Div. Hohenstaufen were together with other small units operating around Berhida, Papkezsi, Soly and Vilonya. They were involved in heavy fighting in an attempt to stop the Russian offensive and to keep the corridor out of the Jenö pocket open. From here, the 1. Pz. Div, 44 Inf. Div. and 5. SS Pz. Div. Wiking broke out during the night of 22-23 March 1945 along with the remnants of other units.

I couldn't find any other German tank units documented in this area, were we getting closer? Could AJ9 be from either 1. or 9. SS Pz. Div.? I contacted a couple of fellow historians who specialise in I. SS.Pz. Korps and the authors of "Duel in the mist" but none of them could recall seeing a turret number combination like AJ9 within I. SS.Pz.Korps. Therefore, I was left with 9. SS.Pz.Div. Hohenstaufen.

Unexpectedly a couple of photos appeared on eBay, showing a SS Pz.IV H at Tarnopol in April 1944, it carried the turret numbers AJ9! After a quick search, I soon discovered that the Waffen-SS unit operating in Tarnopol in April 1944 was...9. SS. Pz.Div Hohenstaufen!

In front of the AJ9 Pz.IV picture stood SS-Ostuf. Bauer who was the adjutant to the commander of the SS Pz.Rgt 9, Otto Meyer. I figured that now the code was cracked; AJ stood for Adjutant and 9 for SS. Pz.Rgt 9. The commander of SS-Pz.Rgt 9 had KO9 on its turret (Kommandant SS-Pz.Rgt 9) - it makes sense doesn't it?

I was also fortunate to receive the original copy of the AJ9 Panther photo from a Russian contact, together with many other photos from the Balaton book along with several unpublished photos.

In January 2009 the research team decided to investigate the area we had visited earlier and with new information they first set off to Papkeszi and Peremarton. They would be looking for the location of Hummel 113 where the local historian in Balatonfüzfö claimed was photographed. After some searching they found the spot and could make a then and now comparison. Bingo! Now the hunt for AJ9 was really getting hot. The team continued to Berhida and once again met a familiar face - the local historian I had met a few months earlier. After my visit, he had been thinking about the picture of AJ9 and now believed it could be found in Kiralyszentistvan, between Hajmasker and Vilonya. The team immediately set of to visit this area, but once there nothing matched. They went back to Vilonya and after parking the car they went for a short walk along the old road to Papkeszi...suddenly they began to see houses that looked familiar. After a closer investigation they realised they have found the location of AJ9! They visited the neighbour's house (to the right in the photo) and met a lady who said that her grandfather lived in one of the houses as a young kid. He was visiting at the time and came out of the house to talk to the team. To begin with, he could not remember anything but slowly his memories come back.

Let us first hear what the team say a about this fortunate day:

....Start at 6 am 11.01.09 from Budapest, me and my brother, by car. Istvan started at the same time but from Győr. We reached the area from Szekesfehervar direction, M7 highway to Balatonkenese, than go to Papkeszi, short check from the car, mainly the roofs, and the fences. No solution, go towards to Cholorchemia, and than go north to the meeting point with Istvan in the entrance of the Peremarton factory area. We met there approx. 9 am. Park the car, and then go on foot inside the factorial area. The first old man we met told that he knows the hummel road. What a fortune?!!!!. We were in the right road, but a bit further from the exact spot. We found the place in the next few minutes. Taken photos, check the similarities, the typical old brick fence's corner. It was 100% right. The next step, how to find the AJ9. We started to strangling around, we tried to find some local people. We talked to a lot of locals, but there wasn't any useful information, except the fact, Peremarton hasn't got a house like in our photo (AJ9). The only advice was, go to Berhida, check there. Let us go back to the cars, first we made a short visit in Cholorchemia, this is small village between Papkeszi and Peremarton. It was builted for the factory workers, and it existed in the wartime. No solution. Go towards to Berhida. There we met a lot of people, but they couldn't gave any closer information, except, there was no KO'd german panzer in the town during march/april. There

The team that found AJ9. Istvan, Mirko and Otto, Mirko is holding scrap metal from AJ9 found in the garden.

Mr. Veleg was a young boy who lived in Vilonya, across the street from where AJ9 was blown up and was an eyewitness to events in 1945.

Mr. Veleg gives valuable information about the fate of AJ9 to the author during a visit to his old home in Vilonya where his daughter lives today.

A computer match of then and now pictures gives an astonishing result. There was no longer any doubt that the author had found the exact location were AJ9 was blown up by its crew. Note the house to the far right, where Mr. Veleg lived in 1945.

was the old man, Mirko met before, he said he know where is our Panther place. He gave us an advice; check Királyszentistván, the first house next to the road from Vilonya. We went there, to check that, but there wasn't any similar house, and the terrain was quite different as seen on our photo. Then a short discussion with Mirko (via phone) and Istvan how to continue. Go to Vilonya was the order. We reached Vilonya, from Királyszentistván, and we found the old Papkeszi road, in the southwestern border of the village. Park down the car, spoke with the locals, but no info's. We started to walk through the street, and we found the house not far from our parking place and a man came out and told us about the Panther picture...he lived as a young kid next to the house behind the Panther AJ 9....

Vilonya is typical picturesque little village in the Veszprem county and had a population of approximately 600 in 1945. Vilonya was caught in the middle of the fighting in March 1945 but luckily, the village suffered little damage during the fighting.

In April 2009 I returned to Hungary and met up with the team to visit Vilonya, so that I could interview the old man who had lived there as a young boy. Today he lives in a hospital but he was happy to return to Vilonya to meet us. His very enthusiastic daughter who now lived in the neighbouring house picked him up. The old man had kept his wartime memories and was happy to talk to us and re-live the events that took place over 60 years ago. We were offered an overwhelming lunch, sitting there eating a genuine Hungarian meal and local wine surrounded by the old buildings remains a very strong memory for me.

The old man, Sandor Velegy, lived in the house seen to the right in the picture of AJ9 where he and his family made a living as farmers with a small number of livestock. He remembers the intense activity in March 1945; the Germans had a communication centre and a FLAK or Artillery unit in his garden. Like most young boys, he was very curious and once he had accidently ruined a German radio antenna when he came too close with his horse cart, the German troops were naturally furious and gave him verbal roasting! The Staff unit was probably 9.SS.

Pz.Dv. Hohenstaufen, and the spot was well chosen as it gives a good overview of the area. Mr Velegy remembers that the Panther (AJ9) stood in the opposite garden for several days before it was blown up, but he never dared to approach it as the front rapidly came closer to the village. On the evening of March 22 Mr. Sandor left the village, taking the cows and oxen with him, trying to find a safer area for them in Balatonfüzfö as the Russians were approaching. He left Vilonya on a horse cart, with the cattle following behind. However, he lost all the animals during the chaotic night along the road, full of refugees and retreating soldiers trying to move west. When he returned to Vilonya the following morning, the 23rd, which was his birthday, the Panther was already blown up. The communications and mechanical personnel were getting ready to leave and the Russians stood just outside Vilonya. The Germans explained to Mr. Velegy that the Panther had been blown up during the night and that the crew had left on a truck. Judging from the photo of AJ 9 the crew had probably tried to refuel during the night but failed to do so, maybe because the lack of fuel.

When the last Germans had left Vilonya, T-34's from the 20. Guards Tank Brigade rolled into the village and unfortunately the people were exposed to looting and physical violence. The main target for the looters was the livestock and peoples personal possessions. This is of course not just a Russian phenomenon; all armies carried it out during the war.

AJ9 stood in the village for some time and a Russian team evaluated it and gave it number 111. It was later partially scrapped but the hull was probably towed to the train station in Balatonfüzfö. One story says that an old man took the rubber from the wheels and made use of it for his bicycle, but one has to wonder how that would have worked out and no trace of such a thing could be found in the village.

Another Panther was blown up near Varga mill in Vilonya at approximately the same time, not far from AJ9's location. It could possibly have been from the staff of 9.SS. Pz.Rgt. as the location is not far from AJ9's and lies on the route to Papkeszi in one direction and Vilonya in the other. We were not able to investigate this location during our trip; the landowner was anything but welcoming towards us and literally told us to bugger off. Other enthusiasts had been here before us, searching for souvenirs etc. The Panther at Varga mill was later identified as 112.

The house behind AJ9 in the photo from 1945 was owned by the local station master who worked at the small train station in Vilonya. His name was Takács Janos and he was also a part time farmer. The lean to building was used for drying corn and was not torn down until 1968, even today there are still cracks from the explosion in the wall of the main building. Today a family who left Budapest for a life in the countryside, live in

This aerial map from 1952 shows the Vilonya area.

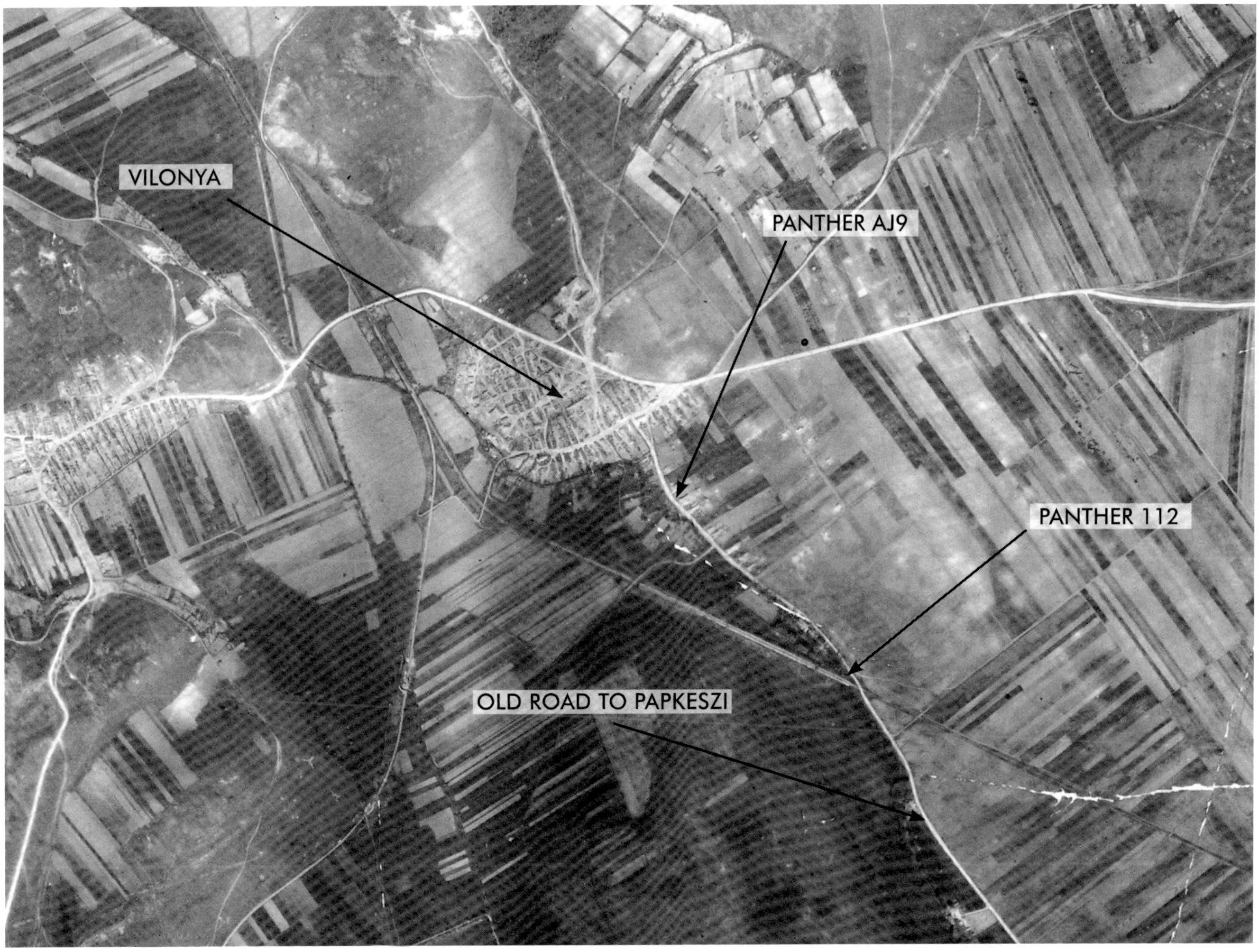

Max K. via Mirko Bayerl

Panther 112 was photographed at Varga Mill in Vilonya, approximately 300 meters from AJ9. Like AJ9, it was blown up by its crew on the night of 22-23 March. Parts from this tank have been found recently, confirming the location. 9.SS Pz.Div. Hohenstaufen had a few survivors with zimmerit that made it through from Arnhem and the Ardennes that were then finally deployed in Hungary, 112 was one of them.

→

The spot today is nearly unchanged, and the road and the hills in the background helped identifying it.

Bildarchiv Preussischer Kulturbesitz

After an extremely thorough and careful examination of this Panther photograph, then comparing it to the photograph of evaluation number 112 by several Panther specialists, we came to the conclusion that this was the same Panther. The M.N.H zimmerit pattern matched perfectly along with the small section of zimmerit missing from the upper edge of the glacis in front of the radio operator's hatch and the area around the kugelblende. The camouflage that can be made out in both photographs also matches, particularly the section of light paint on the gun travel lock, which given the age of this vehicle are almost certainly sections of disc camouflage. It probably belonged to the adjutant of the I./SS.Pz.Rgt.9. It is passing an unidentified Wehrmacht unit using SwS half tracks in the St Vith area of the Ardennes in December 1944. It was later photographed at Varga Mill in Vilonya in March 1945. The wrecks above were very well known to locals who remember playing in them as children before they was towed away to be scrapped.

the small lot where AJ 9 was blown up. We were kindly invited to scan the ground with metal detectors in search of traces of AJ 9. The father of the family followed our work with great interest, despite the fact that we dug numerous holes in his yard, we did indeed find some scap metal from AJ 9!

It was a sunny day in March, and after a ten year search I had finally found the location of AJ9, its story, an eye witnesses from the war, and even some souvenirs. My trips to Hungary were such extraordinary adventures in many ways and I will probably visit Vilonya again. Looking back, I realise that Hummel 113 turned out to be the key to solving the mystery of AJ9. Thanks to the piece of wall in the background of the photo we were able to find the right area to continue our search. One of the team members recalls:

...I think that without the location of Hummel no. 113 we would not have been able to find the AJ9. Our theory was absolutely right, to make a cornerstone from the Peremarton 113 Hummel. From that point of view, this story has two „stars". And if I think further, the main evidence was the brick corner behind the Hummel! If we had not located the Hummel, we would not have any hope to find AJ9 that day. I know the Hummel is not the main subject of this story, but it is a good example of how things can be connected in battle field research, and how each puzzle piece is important....

Without the help of my fantastic friends in the research team I would never have found AJ9, and my deepest gratitude goes to them as well as the Velegy family and their neighbours in Vilonya, who made this search so much more personal.

The team and I have continued our "quest" to indentify vehicles and locations in the Balaton area, more mysteries have been solved with lots of similar memorable stories along the way. However, that is another story, and maybe there will be another model after AJ 9 too.

Finally, I would like to thank AMC and Stefan De Meyer for the permission to use some of their pictures in this article as well as Rüdiger Warnick and Kocsis Istvan for their additional help.

The "AJ9 team" was mainly made up by: Tóth István, Józsa Otto, Peter Barnaky, and my self. Again, thank you all!

Mirko Bayerl

In this photograph we can see that this Panther had a "Sternantenne D" fitted to the normal Antennenfuss used for the vehicles FuG 5 radio. Despite this, it is extremely unlikely that this is a field expedient Befehlspanther for the following reasons: While the "sternantenne D" was normally used with the more powerful FuG 8 radio set that was part of the radio equipment of a Befehlspanther, it could be used in place of a 2 meter rod antenna. This would result in reduced performance for the FuG 5 as a specific rectifier was in place to correct the imbalance between the radio and the antenna for the Fug 5 and the 2m antenna. Furthermore, a FuG 8 set was highly unlikely to have used the standard Antennenfuss on a Panther as this radio needed a large porcelain insulator due to the very high wattage and voltage that this set required to work and would have been extremely hazardous to both the vehicle and crew. There was a very real risk that if not grounded properly that it could cause the fuel load to ignite. Finally, there is no secondary antenna mounted on the turret without which the turret radio equipment could not be installed. Unlike Panther AJ9 which was a purpose built Befehlspanther assembled for this purpose by M.A.N, this Panther is a standard tank that is being used by the battalion staff which is borne out by the Gliderung for this unit in late 1944 and early 1945. It should be noted that the replacement of antennas was a frequent task for the crews, as the antennas were often damaged during battle and transport in rough terrain.

PART 2:

9. SS PZ.DIV.HOHENSTAUFEN AND AJ9 IN HUNGARY

In this text, I would like to trace and document the events of Panther 'AJ9' up to the night of March 23rd 1945, when it was blown up by its crew. I will focus on the Hohenstaufen Division and Panther 'AJ9', as it would be an enormous task to try to describe the whole of "Operation Frühlingserwachen". This account is based on a lot of original research material; I will try to give a vivid description based on facts, instead of an academic disquisition. I have visited all the places mentioned in the text, walked in the fields where it all happened and I have collected maps from that area. I have studied the geographically difficult terrain and plodded the muddy fields during a trip in March and have come to understand the difficulties that all sides involved in this conflict were faced with; Germans, Russians and Hungarians alike.

To trace the movements of Hohenstaufen Division and the exact route of Panther 'AJ9' between 2nd and 23rd of March 1945 has not been easy. Heersgruppe Süd and the different armies sometimes experienced difficulties knowing the exact location of the divisions under their command at a specific point in time. This was caused by not only the sometime contradictory orders issued by different commands, but also the conflict between the Waffen SS and Wehrmacht tactical and strategic doctrine. Both organizations accused each other of making serious errors during the war and after it, but I will not go into that here. I will not focus on exact dates and times, or try to describe the whole operation with all the armies and divisions involved in it. Instead, I will adapt my story to fit into the theme of this book's main purpose, to act as an inspiration to modellers who want to create dioramas and vignettes of the desperate battles in Hungary.

I would like to thank Ian Michael Wood, Otto Jozsa, Martin Block and Kamen

Nevenkin for sharing all of their fantastic information, and their enormous support.

Early March 1945

Transport train after transport train arrives at Komarom railway station by the Donau, on this gray, murky day in March 1945. The same scene is taking place by the city of Raab. Tanks, SPW's and trucks carefully roll off the loading ramps and clutter the railway depot along with thousands of soldiers trying to find their units. The screeching, puffing steam engines, officers yelling commands and vehicle engines echoing in the depot create a scene of incredible chaos to anyone casually observing. Crews and maintenance personnel wave and direct the tanks and armoured vehicles off the flatbed railway wagons. Sleet starts to fall while more trains arrive and daylight is slowly fading. It is busy as grenadiers, tank crews and other troops are quartered in the village and the surrounding area. An entire panzer division has arrived the 9 SS Pz.Div. Hohenstaufen, commanded by SS Oberführer Sylvester Stadler.

The 9 SS Pz.Div. Hohenstaufen belongs to II SS Pz. Korps along with 2 SS Pz.Div. Das Reich has arrived in Hungary to participate in the very last large scale German offensive of the war. Neither officers or enlisted men have any idea of what is going to happen next, only that they have ended up in Hungary instead of the Berlin area that had been expected. Rumours suggest that there will be a secret operation and diversion, the units involved have been given new titles in order to mask their true identity during the preparation for the offensive, the 9 SS Pz.Div. Hohenstaufen has been named "Ausbildungsgruppe Süd"; all markings on the vehicles must be over painted; cuff bands removed, nothing must remain that might reveal the divisions true identity prior to the beginning of the offensive. All measures possible are taken to deceive the Russians regarding preparations' for a forthcoming offensive.

The division has been re equipped quickly from the bitter fighting in the Belgian Ardennes; however, this was achieved with a large contingent of new recruits drafted

AMC

A crossroad south of Komarom. Wehrmach soldiers curiously watches as a SS unit passes on their way to their last offensive, "Frühlingserwachen". Traffic jams were common as the heavy traffic could only be transported on the roads. The white wash on the vehicles are probably still left over from the battle in the Ardennes.

The first elements of SS. Pz.Rgt 9 Hohenstaufen is approaching Seregelyes and the assembly area for the vast operation "Frühlingserwachen". The Pz. IV, passing a knocked out Russian 7,62 cm anti tank gun, is a veteran of the Ardennes fighting of December 1944 and January 1945.

MNZS

in from the Kriegsmarine and Luftwaffe ground personnel with no battle experience and almost no further training. Tanks and other armoured vehicles have been repaired and transported back to the front, after the costly Ardennes offensive.

Arriving in Komarom

The staff of SS Pz.Rgt. 9 Hohenstaufen along with the I Abt. arrives at Komarom in the beginning of March. They began the move down South to the assembly area for the attack around the Seregelyes area. This involves a 70km motorized march along the Kisber – Mor – Stuhlweissenburg main road and they set off the night that they arrived in Komarom or the following morning. The bad weather has made the roads slippery and muddy, making the march troublesome for the column of Panthers, Jagdpanzers, Panzer IV's, Jagdpanthers and other vehicles. Snow, rain and strong winds slow the movement, the poor visibility forces the Russian air force to remain on the ground. However, experience on the Western Front has created a constant fear of air attack, troop movements are mostly conducted at night. This results in road congestion that sometimes comes to total standstill. When dawn breaks, the vehicles are sometimes too close for comfort on the narrow main road. Russian reconnaissance aircraft fly at high altitude, but no ground attack planes are present yet. Panther 'AJ9' is slowly labouring forward somewhere in the extended column.

The other parts of the division exiting Raab, including II SS Pz.Rgt 9, moves slowly, the roads throng with refugees along with other Waffen SS and Wehrmacht units moving towards their assembly points. 1 SS Pz.Div, 12 SS.Pz.Div, 3 Kav.Brig. and 44.Inf.

MNZS

Max.K via Mirko Bayerl

A company commander is giving instructions to the crew of a command Jagdpanzer IV L/70 from 9. SS.Pz.Div. Hohenstaufen, sitting in a muddy field. Driving through the muddy bottom less spring fields was a very risky business, often ending up with a stuck vehicle.

This Panther is a clear example of what could happen, and it was clearly getting nowhere and the recovery possibilities were small. In this situation the tanks were easy targets for the Russians. Note that the cleaning rods are assembled and lays along the side of the hull.

Div HuD. are forced to share the same narrow roads, those who try to cross the fields sink in bottomless sludge and grind to a halt. However, the Hohenstaufen division is accustomed to these hardships since Tarnopol and Ardennes in 1944.

9 SS Pz.Div. Hohenstaufen is one of the 10 Armoured divisions from both Waffen SS and Wehrmacht which has been thrown in as a desperate move to take initiative on the southern part of the eastern front, and further secure the oil fields on the west shore of Lake Balaton and if it proceeds as planned to recapture the oil fields at Ploesti.

This would be a massive offensive; Hitler was obsessed with oil, hence this operation threw his best and last effective armoured units into the battle. The final result however was the collapse of the front and irreconcilable losses for the German units involved. The status of SS Pz.Rgt 9 on the 1st of March 1945 was the following:

- Rgt.Stab.Kp : 1 Panther , 1 PzIV L
- I.Abt . Stabs.Komp : 2 Panther - Total for Befehls-panther in the regiment is given as now only 2, so 1 of the 2 tanks in the Abt Stabskp must have been a Standard Panther.
- 1.KP : 13 Panther
- 2.Kp. : 13 Panther
- 3.Kp : 12 Panther
- 4 Kp : 10 Jagdpanther
- II.Abt Stabkp. 2 Befehls.Pz IV 5 FLAKpz IV Möbelwagen
- 5 Kp : 14 Pz.IV (apparently including a platoon of Pz IV/70 (V))
- 6.Kp : 15 Pz.IV (apparently including a platoon of Pz.IV/70 (V))
- 7.Kp : 13 Stug III
- 8.Kp :13 Stug III
- 9 Kp : 15 Pz.IV /70 (V)

We can see that no Pz.Jg.Abt was attached to the Hohenstaufen; instead, it had a ninth

MNZS

Nádasdladany then and now. A StuG III G from 7. or 8. /SS.Pz. Rgt. 9 Hohenstaufen has broken down and is being towed away westwards from the battle area by a late production FAMO. This village was defended by Hohenstaufen around the 20th March. According to the original caption, the smoke in the background is the result of an air attack.

company equipped with Pz IV/L70(V). The numbers given here are the theoretical strength if the vehicles had all been fully operational. However the true number of armoured vehicles available for combat operations was 13 Panthers, 17 Pz IV's, 15 StuG IIIs and 19(10) JgPz L/70(V). The rest being under repair at the field workshops close to the front line. Extensively damaged vehicles or those in need of repairs that are more complicated were sent back to Germany, Austria or were transported to Hajmasker near Veszprem. Most vehicles were returned to the front, but there was a constant stream of damaged vehicles being repaired in the workshops. This ultimately meant that there were always more vehicles under repair than those available for combat operations at the front.

I Abt. received a total of 58 Panthers in November and early December 1944. These had solid white numbers painted on the rear turret quarter, the Jagdpanthers had their numbers painted towards the rear of the fighting compartment.

II.Abt received their 30 Pz IVs in November 1944, 28 Stug IIIs was delivered to the division in November 1944, with an additional 5 in February 1945. A number of JgdPz IV/70 (V) were delivered in November 1944 with 12 more in February 1945. There were also some 120 Sd.Kfz 251 SPW's of different versions and 42 light SPW's in operational order. Of course there were also recovery vehicles like the Bergepanther and 18tone Zugkraftwagen in the units inventory. The Artillery Regiments used both Hummel's and Wespes. All in all, the division contained circa 17.000 men all told, the actual number of fighting men was naturally considerably less.

The most plausible scenario would be that Panther AJ9, being the only Befehlspanther in the I Abt. Staff company, was used by the commander of I Abt.; SS Sturmbannführer Magnus Flor, the other Panther, which was a standard Panther was used by his adjutant. AJ9 was originally the Adjutants vehicle but was taken over by Flor following the losses in the Ardennes. Magnus Flor was killed in action somewhere near Lake Balaton in March 1945; probably a few days after the crew had blown up 'AJ9

9 SS Pz.Div. finally reaches its assembly point at Seregelyes and establish their headquarters in the farm estate of Bolondvari Tanya, half-way between Seregelyes and Belsöbarand. The division is exhausted after the hardship encountered during the march, and the divisional commander asks his superiors to give the division time to assemble and regroup before the attack, but this is not granted. The grenadiers from SS Pz.Gren.Rgt's 19 and 20 begin the assault on March 6 after a short artillery barrage. Tanks and other AFV's remains in the assembly area as they cannot follow the grenadiers over the muddy terrain, 'AJ9' along with many other AFV's remains at headquarters or inside Seregelyes. However, parts of I Abt are moving towards Sarosd along with the main road under the command of SS Obersturmbannführer Eberhard Telkamp, commander of SS Pz.Rgt.9. The left flank is open because of the difficult terrain, 3 Panzer Division who were tasked to advance on Hohenstaufens flank were hampered by muddy fields and destroyed bridges which, coupled with heavy resistance encountered later near Mihaly Major, delayed their arrival and ensured that they never kept pace with Hohenstaufen as planned. This left the flank towards Hohenstaufen fully exposed. On the right flank, 2 SS Pz.Div. Das Reich advanced and reached positions at Heinrich Major (see "The Search for AJ9').

The Hohenstaufen reached the area north west of Sarosd and dig defensive positions. Their padded uniforms are wet from rain and mud and the soldiers are completely exhausted. They have no armoured support, as these are still static in Seregelyes and around the headquarters (Bolondvari Tanya). Any attempt to move out into the wide, open fields usually results in the vehicles becoming bogged down or being forced to return to their original positions. At the same time the Das Reich division is engaged in heavy fighting at Heinrich Major and has failed to make any headway. When the Russians break through and begin "Operation Wien" to the north

Although the picture is of bad quality, we can see evidence of the hard battle fought around Papkeszi Station. The ground is littered with many wrecks, both German and Russian. The picture at the bottom shows the station area today.

Mirko Bayerl Collection

of Stuhlweissenburg on March 16/17 1945, part of this operation is a massive attack started by the 18. Tank Corps on the Hohenstaufen's positions. SS Pz.Div Das Reich leave their positions together with the 6. Panzer Divsion and the 356 Infantry Division and head north to new positions around the Kisber - Komarom area. The Hohenstaufen starts to withdraw from the positions that they had occupied around Sarosd, they withdraw in an orderly manner to ensure that the area of the front that they are responsible for does not collapse. The Panzer Regiment along with Panther 'AJ9' moves out from Seregelyes, they had to travel on very poor country roads via the villages of Bolondvari Tanya, Belsöbarand and Föveny Psz to the Szabadbattyan area. The shattered division is then thrown in to a violent battle along the Nádasdládány line as the Russians breaks through in the north and east. This is where 'AJ9' engages in bitter fighting, there are no longer any distinct combat formations. The divisions regiments, battalions and companies fight where they are ordered to. However, on many occasions orders are not needed, the Russians are advancing from all directions and the divisions troops are forced to defend themselves without reference to an overall strategy. The division is pushed west slowly, both SS Pz.Gren.Rgt 19 and 20 have suffered enormous losses as have the Pz.Rgt. Burning SPW's, Panthers and Panzer IV's together with Russian T34's litter the landscape. The ground is black from shell impacts and the sky is filled with smoke. The weather has improved so that now low flying Russian aircraft begin to attack day and night and causes heavy losses for the Germans despite the German and Hungarian air forces counterattack and attempts support the ground forces.

On March 21st, I Abt has only eleven operational Panthers. The Russians seize Varpalota and Hajmasker after bitter fighting with 1 SS Pz.Div Leibstandarte Adolf Hitler (LAH) and move rapidly west and south. More Russian forces push from the south and many German formations run the risk of being trapped in a cauldron around Polgardi. 1 PzDiv and 5 SS.Pz.Div. Wiking, 3 Pz.Div, 44 Inf.Div and s.Pz.Abt 509 are concentrated together with smaller units and "Kampfgruppen" and run a very serious risk of being surrounded and trapped here. A breakthrough of these formations, before they were encircled took place during the night of 22nd & 23rd March from the Jenö area, this subsequently became known as the break out from the Jenö pocket. This outbreak was possible thanks to the efforts of the Hohenstaufen division and the 4 Kav. Div who kept the corridor open at the north. The southern side of this corridor, which was only a few kilometres wide, was held by the 23. Pz.Div and the 3.Kav. Div. along with other smaller units, who held a line from Balatonkenese via Csajag to Polgardi. The losses for the withdrawing units are terrible; only some 1500 men made it through and were gathered at Balatonfüzfö. An example of this is that SS Pz.Div Wiking lost or were forced to abandon almost all their tanks and armoured vehicles on the fields just south of Nádasdládány and Jenö. The countryside was a testament to this human tragedy; there were bogged down, abandoned and destroyed armoured vehicles littering the landscape along with hundreds of other vehicles, horses and fallen soldiers. Horrendous scenes like those from the "Falaise pocket" in France in August 1944, are again taking place.

The next few days finds the Hohenstaufen involved in heavy fighting around south Ösi and Berhida.

"Obersturmfürer Telkamps Panzers attacked at all Schwerpunkts of the division and again and again brought relief to the hard fighting Pz.grenadiers" (Wilhelm Tieke).

According to some sources, 15 Josef Stalin tanks are supposed to have been knocked out by eight Jagdpanthers from 4/ SS Pz.Rgt 9 just east of Berhida The divisions units are pushed further and further to the west towards Papkeszi and the surrounding area, despite the attempts to halt the Russian onslaught. Berhida is lost. 'AJ9' has already withdrawn to Vilonya via Papkeszi prior to these events.

Der Letzte Kampf - Das Panzer Duell

The Hohenstaufen division had built a makeshift defence system from the Berhida area around the village of Papkeszi and its railway station towards Vilonya. The headquarters are in Kastely Major beside the old road between Papkeszi and Vilonya. The tanks of I Abt are placed in defensive

The author overlooks the plains towards Peremarton and Berhida. In this old vinyard, large elements of SS.Pz.Rgt 9 dug in, awaitig the Russian attack. Visible in the background is the road where the Russian 20th and 22nd Guards Tank Brigade attacked and suffered heavy losses.

Clearly visible here, are the trenches where the FLAK unit mentioned in the article had it´s positions. The trenches were re-used from the earlier battles during the winter. The team searches for equipment and other evidence of battle in the ground, and some very interesting discoveries were made.

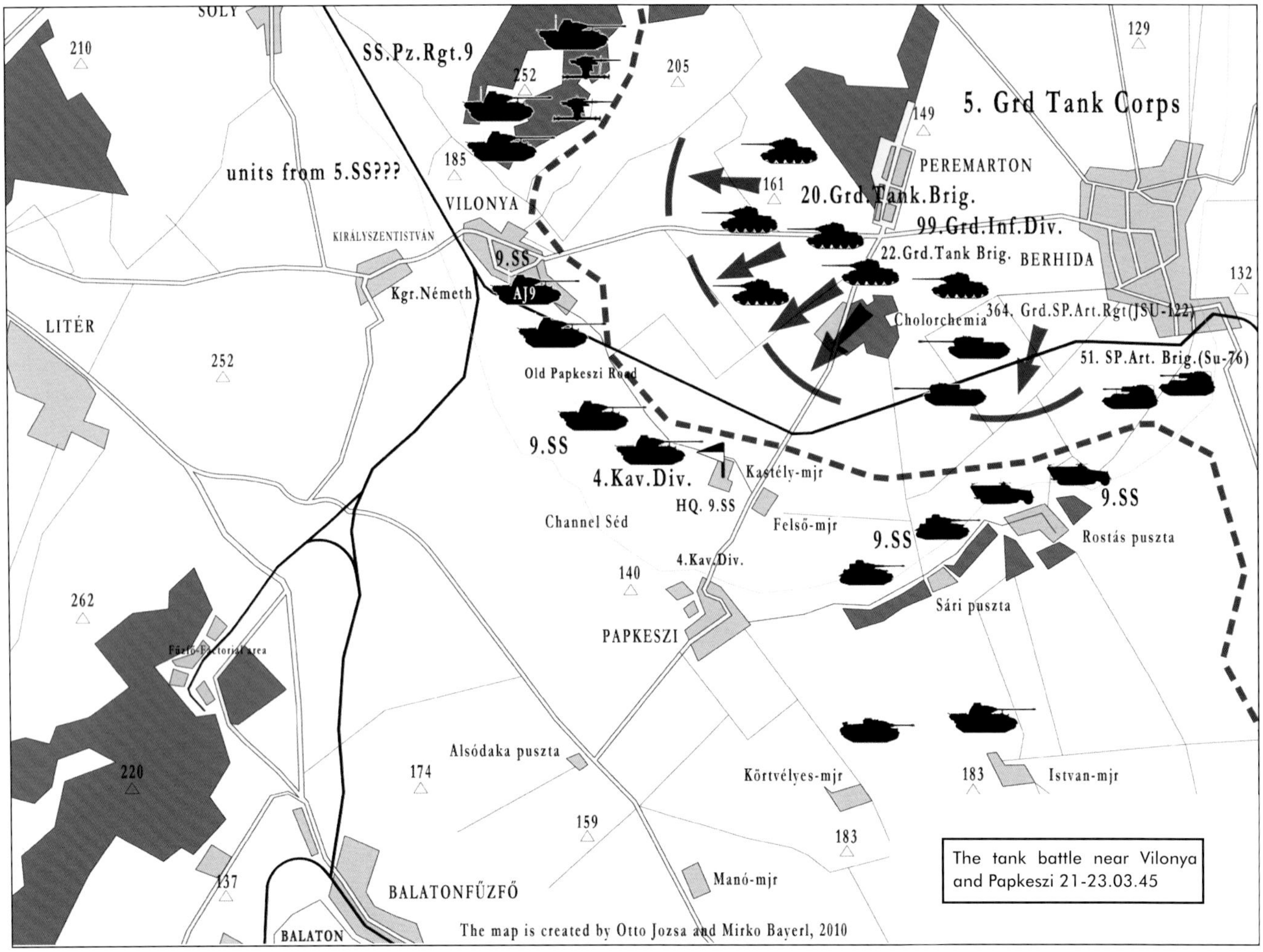

The tank battle near Vilonya and Papkeszi 21-23.03.45

positions between Vilonya and Papkeszi, with a railway embankment acting as natural shelter eastwards. The majority of I Abt. SS.Pz.Rgt 9 dig in and camouflage their vehicles in a vineyard just north east of Vilonya. FLAK units and SS Grenadiers roll forward and utilize old emplacements from the fighting that had previously taken place here in December 1944 January 1945. Tank crews and grenadiers are preparing for battle along the old Vilonya to Papkeszi road. 'AJ9' has left the headquarters in Kastely Major at Papkeszi, it has marched along the old road to Vilonya and stops in the garden of a house, which the rest of the staff together with a battery from SS Pz.Art. Rgt 9 had moved into prior to their arrival. 'AJ9' is takes up a tactically good position while some of the villagers prepare to leave. Horses are harnessed to wooden hay carts, which in turn are loaded with the necessities and the family's valuables.

The commanders Telkamp and Flor use AJ9 to communicate with divisional headquarters. They attempt to organize a sound defensive perimeter together with 4 Kav.Div who were stationed at Papkeszi. Other elements of Hohenstaufen and its II Abt SS Pz.Rgt 9 with Pz IVs, StuGs and Jg.PzIV (V) L/70s stand directly south of Berhida.

SS-obersturmbannführer Telkamp :

"While Regiements 19 and 20, battle south of Berhida to hold open the kessel. an Abteilung of the Pz.Rgt (I.Abt) secures the open flank of the division to the north against any surprise armoured thrusts by the enemy, which were the order of the day at that time. The position is carefully chosen in a vineyard, from which there is good visibility of the entire foreground. The Panzers are ,naturally impeccably camouflaged, even the track marks are covered with leaves and branches. The men are particular in their assignments and make good use of all possibilities. Each knows his job to the last dot"

The Hohenstaufen now has a perfect overview and control over both roads leading from Berhida and Peremarton. The division has not fully regrouped; some shattered units are stuck behind Russian lines at Ösi. Suddenly the Russians launch their assault, led by the 5 Guards Tank Corps (6 Guard Tank Army) under General Saveliev's command. Russian 20 and 22 Guards Tank Brigade, assaults Peremarton, Papkeszi and Vilonya. They are supported by 364 Guards Heavy Self Propelled Gun Rgt, with some twenty ISU 122s and twenty SU 76s from 51 Art SP Brigade covering the flanks.

Mirko Bayerl Collection

General Saveliev, commander of the 5th Guards Tank Corps.

The Russian spearhead with some seventy T34s with infantry riding on the engine decks or running alongside. Peremarton

Ullstein Bild

SS Grenadierers seeking cover in the Berhida / Papkeszi area, preparing for the next attack from Russian armour and attack aircraft. They belong to either SS. Pz Gr.Rgt 19 or 20 and are all wearing the padded camouflage uniforms that were issued early March -45. Many trenches in this area had already been dug during the January battles and were now used agin during the retreat fighting in March.

is overrun by the 20 Guards Tank Brigade (Colonel Zhilin) and they then continue towards Vilonya. Meanwhile 22 Guard Tank Brigade (Colonel Ostapenko) assaults Papkeszi. ISU 122s from the 364 G.H.SP.g Rgt follow at a close distance and SU 76s from the 51 SP-Art.Brigade cover the attack. Infantry from the 99 Guards Rifle Div participate too, and they have apparently not been informed about the dug in and camouflaged Panthers and other AFVs from SS Pz.Rgt 9.

The tank and FLAK crews wait patiently for the T 34s to come in to range. A T34 is immobilized by a mine at a distance of 600 meters, this triggers the order for the german Gunners to open fire. One after another, the Panthers discharge concentrated fire from their 7.5cm guns simultaneously with the FLAK units. This is what the Hohenstaufen tank crews have been waiting for and the enemy is now in dire trouble. Hohenstaufen's own tanks are well disguised in the vineyard and every crew knew in detail what their task was. It must be hell over at the Russian lines, their tanks are burning. The Germans watch as the Russians start to panic. Some AVF's try to get off the roads into the fields, but are soon stuck in the muddy conditions and become easy targets. The Russian infantry tries to find shelter in the open landscape, but to no avail. A large number of T34's are knocked out and many Russian soldiers are killed. Vehicles burn and black smoke covers the area, as the Russian troops turn back in panic towards a large forest area to the north of Peremarton.

As this is taking place, orders are frantically given and received by the crew of AJ9 in Vilonya as the commanders struggle to maintain control of their troops in the maelstrom unfolding before them. Telkamp again :

Our crews wait, tense for the order to fire..when the russians finally are about 600 - 800 meters away, we fire; precisely and rapidly. In a very short the entire herd of enemy tanks is wiped out...

The German reports show that over 100 enemy tanks and SPG's were knocked out together with considerable numbers of Russian troops killed in action in this battle. Russian sources have report lower numbers, but still admit to heavy losses. Of course, the German forces also suffered losses in this battle, a number of Panthers had been knocked out by Russian ISU 122's and SU 76's. However, the greatest loss for the Germans was that they were running out of both ammunition and had used almost all their fuel.

Papkeszi is lost after heavy fighting around the railway station and later, Vilonya meets the same fate. The Russian forces push on relentlessly and the German units are forced to retreat and they are forced to destroy or abandon some of their tanks and heavy equipment because of this.

Locals confirmed after the war, the state of chaos and intensity of the fighting, eyewitness's tell of battle weary and mentally exhausted tank crews during their retreat through Papkeszi. When the Russian forces were on the outskirts of Papkeszi, some of these troops tore off their uniform patches showing their connection to the Waffen SS. One Panther commander, suffering from battle stress and frayed nerves, was offered some food by an ethnic German woman, who tried to calm him down. His anguish was relevant, he was shivering and his dishevelled demeanour left a lasting impression on the young boy who witnessed the scene.

The russians however overt run the Division and took Papkeszi , later Vilonya also was lost//....The troopers and Panzer grenadiers who had been overstressed in body and soul during the hard battles of the last days gave their utmost, but could not hold against the far superior forces of the attacking enemy... (Wilhelm Tieke)

The great Rückmarsch is now a fact. The crew of Panther 'AJ9' searches for fuel but this proves to be futile, now the Russians have reached the outskirts of Vilonya. Early in the morning of March 23rd, the crew decide to blow up the tank, as the crew move west over to Balatonfüzfö in a workshop truck, a deafening explosion which tears off the turret is heard. The remaining parts of the staff units are also preparing for the march; mechanics, signal troops and other units leave Vilonya, along with terrified civilians. Soon the village is quiet, leaving 'AJ9' and all the other vehicles as historical monuments; at least until the T 34's come rattling into the empty village. Vilonya is now in Russian hands, like thousands of Hungarian villages in 1944-45. Some Russian tank crews stop and indifferently watch as 'AJ9' burns, but eventually roll on. A thirteen year old boy curiously watches the events. His name is Sandor Velegy and will tell a story about it all 65 years later.

The Russian steamroller moves on and on, seizes Veszprem, Marko, Nemesvamos and Taploca, and advances further west towards Austria. The Hohenstaufen is shattered into small fighting units and is just like every division, trying to escape the Russian onslaught. In May 1945 the remnants of Hohenstaufen capitulates to the Allies.

Mirko Bayerl

A Jagdpanther from the 4/SS. Pz.Rgt 9 Hohenstaufen, which had around 10 operational Jagdpanthers in early March. Here we can clearly see that the Jagdpanthers also used solid white numbers in the rear part of the vehicle, this one is 401. The small inset picture shows a Jagd Pz. IV L/70, also from Hohenstaufen. Both were abandoned west of Veszprem after the battles in the Vilonya area.

Max K. via Mirko Bayerl

Another Panther from SS.Pz.Rgt 9, this time from the Ardennes. This picture again shows the typical solid white tactical numbers at the rear of the turret, which was very significant for this unit.

Charles C. Dike, Recon Co, 607th TD Bn

Max K. via Mirko Bayerl

Two Panthers - two destinies

This Panther was blown up together with several other tanks in the Veszprem area. It belonged to either 1.SS.Pz.Div LAH or 9.SS.Pz.Div. Hohenstaufen. The fence and the hills in the background helped identifying the spot today.

This Panther G belonged to Ernst Barkmanns Company from 4./ SS.Pz.Rgt 2 Das Reich and carried tactical number 411. Just behind, but not visible stands Panther 423 from the same unit. This was a common sight along the retreat rout towards Austria where neither fuel, spare parts or recovery vehicles were available. Today a modern asphalt road has been laid. Photo taken near Veszprem.

Max K. via Mirko Bayerl

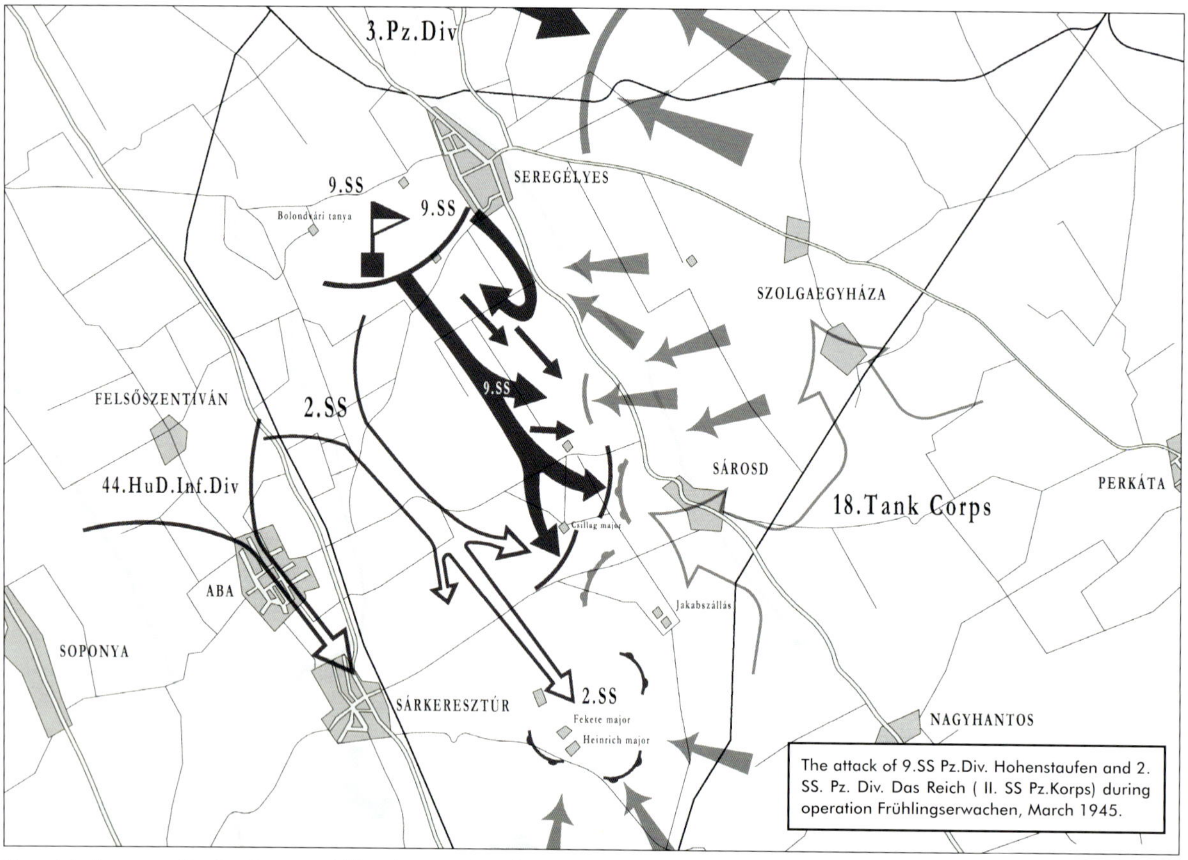

The attack of 9.SS Pz.Div. Hohenstaufen and 2. SS. Pz. Div. Das Reich (II. SS Pz.Korps) during operation Frühlingserwachen, March 1945.

The original map used by the Germans. All locations mentioned in this article can be found.

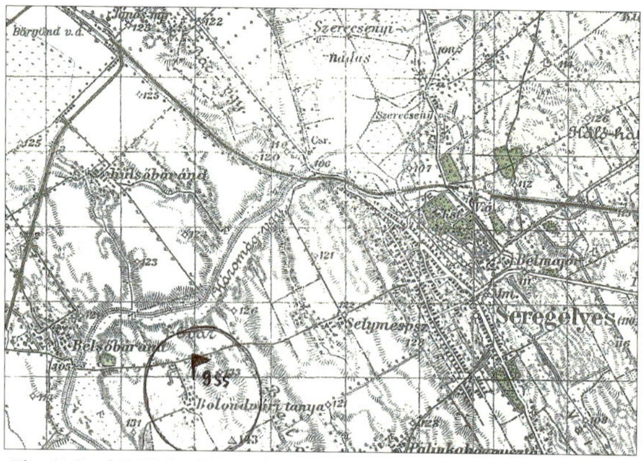

The HQ of 9.SS Pz.Div. Hohenstaufen was at Bolondvári tanya at the beginning of operation Frühlingserwachen in March. AJ 9 was occasionally statined here. Nothing remains of the HQ buildings today.

This was the headquarter of the 9.SS. Pz.Div. Hohenstaufen in Papkeszi. Here the division commander of 5.SS.Pz.Div.Wiking personaly visited the commander of 9.SS to thank him for keeping the Jenö pocket open so they could escape. The building lies on the old road from Papkeszi to Vilonya, so here was AJ9 probably briefing days before it was blown up.

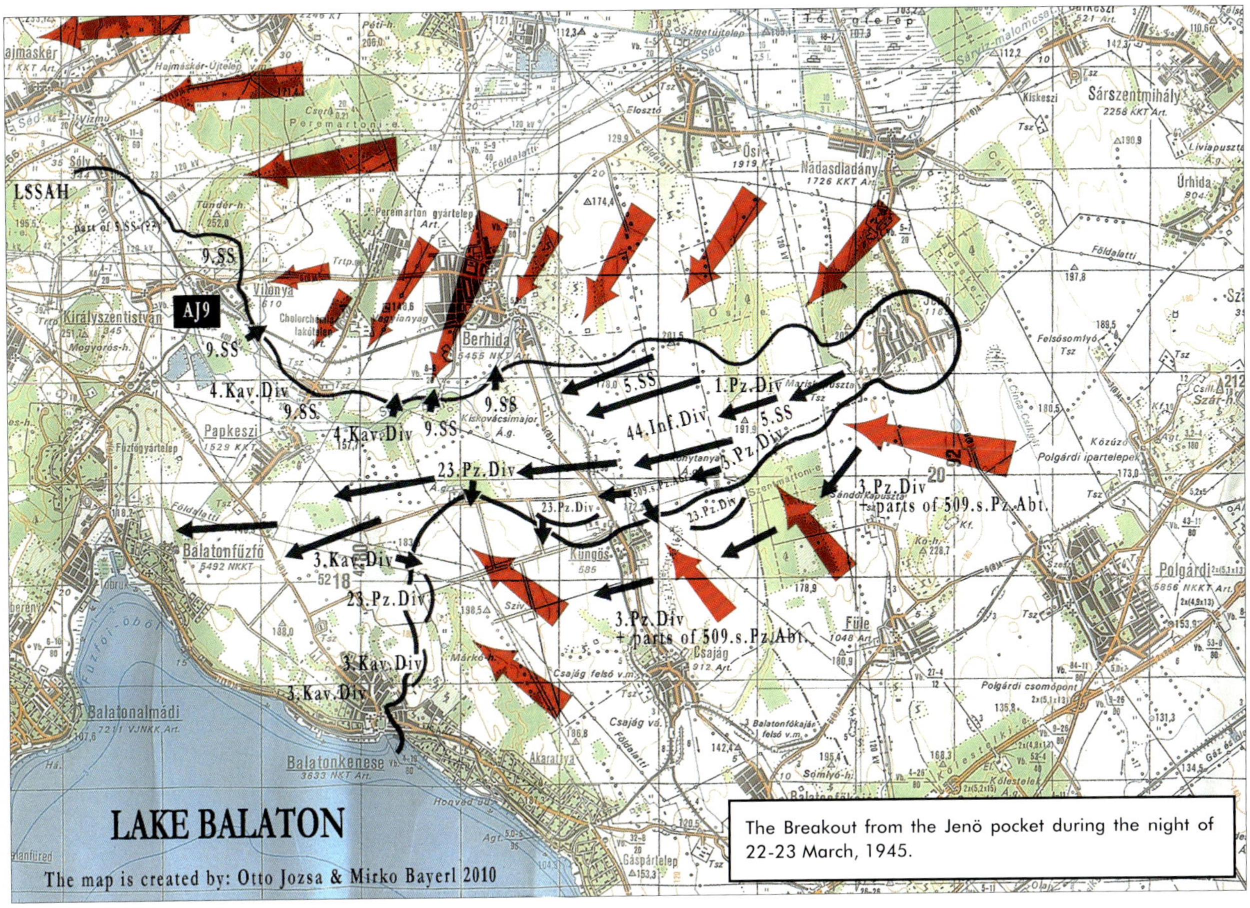

The Breakout from the Jenö pocket during the night of 22-23 March, 1945.

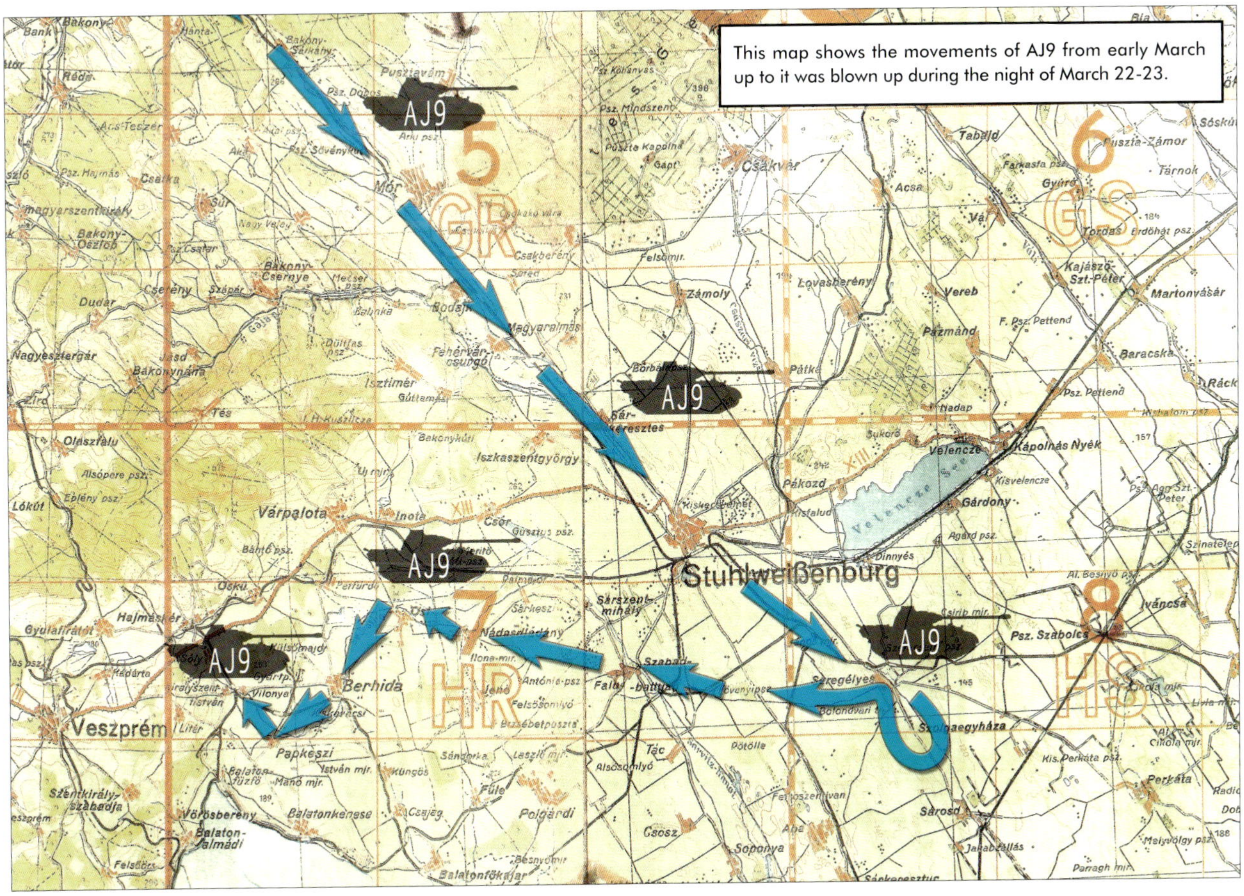

This map shows the movements of AJ9 from early March up to it was blown up during the night of March 22-23.

PART 3: THE AJ9 DIORAMA

MORGENGRAUEN

In the third and final part of his articles, Mirko tells the story of how he created the AJ9 diorama. The goal was to depict a typical countryside village, catching the atmosphere of a cold grey morning in March 1945.

ÜBER PAPKESZI

"DAWN OVER PAPKESZI"

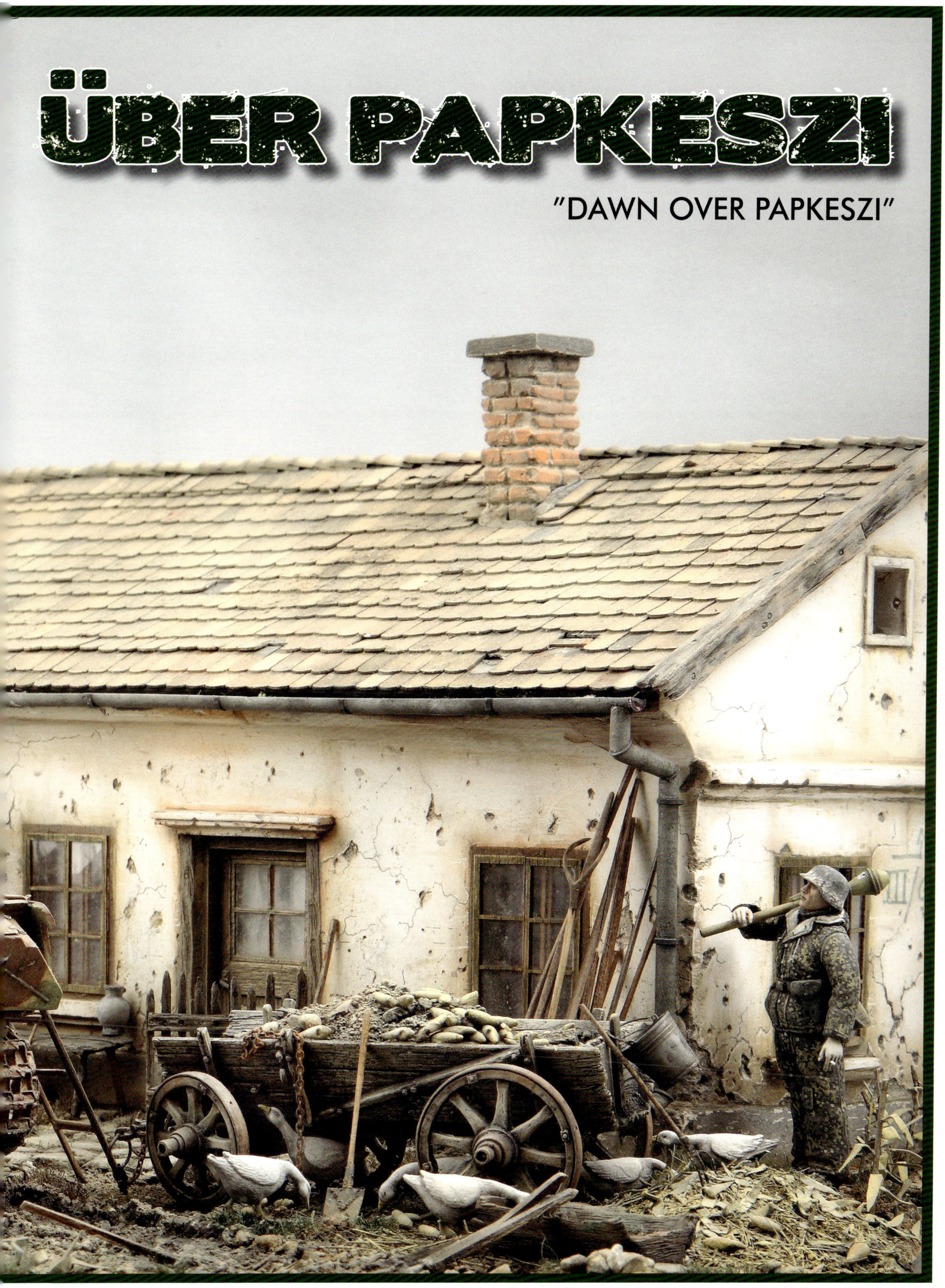

It is a cold morning on March 22nd 1945, the time is 7.00 o'clock, the mist is still lingering over the corn- and sunflower fields. The small hamlet of Papkeszi is eerily quiet and empty and on a withered cornfield outside the village, two T34's and a German StuG III stand, still lightly burning and smoking; knocked out during yesterday's battle. Geese saunter by searching for something to eat on the cold morning, as muted artillery thunders and the faint cracking of machine gun fire is heard in the distance. Now and then, an aeroplane passes by at low altitude; this time it is some Me 109's. The crew of Panther 'AJ 9' has been able to sleep a few hours during the night; something which they have been unable to do during the last few weeks. They are quartered in a small farmhouse, which is an annex to a larger building where units from SS.Pz.Rgt. 9 Hohenstaufen have a makeshift staff and communication centre for the last few days. The tank commander, who is lodged in another house, climbs on to the tank to brief the crew on the previous night's fighting and the orders and tactics for the next few hours of action around Berhida, Vilonya and Papkeszi. On the way to his tank, the commander witnessed a German fighter plane attacking and shooting down a Soviet Sturmovik aircraft, which then crashed somewhere near Lake Balaton. The Russian air activity and ground attacks had been steadily increasing both day and night. The German troops have had a hard time finding shelter from these attacks in the open Hungarian landscape, when the low flying Sturmovik's had appeared. They have sought shelter in farms and their outbuildings, which in Hungarian are called Major, Tanyas or Pusztas depending on the size. The German

Note the writing on the wall; III/.SS-Pz.Gren.Rgt "Germania" (5.SS.Pz.Div Wiking) operated in this area during the battles in January 1945.

and Hungarian air forces activity has been relatively high, but nowhere near that of the Russians'. The crew listens enthusiastically while the commander describes the events; the driver takes a mouthful of the Hungarian wine he has found, but the radio operator has already closed his hatch and is probably setting the radio frequencies for the day.

The family living in the house has fled westwards with their most precious belongings and livestock, just like thousands of other civilians, in an attempt to escape the harrowing battles. Rumours tell of Russian breakthroughs in one village after another, and many know what fate waits for those who have not fled when the Russians come. Only "Nagymama" – Grandmother – chose to stay behind to look after the house and the few animals that could not be brought; she is too old and weak to come along. She is up early and is looking curiously out through the window. Maybe she will offer the soldiers something to eat or drink later on.

The Schwimmwagen, somewhat sheltered in the garage, belongs to the I.Abt. staff. A weary and tired SS Grenadier has appeared from around the corner of the house. He stops when he hears the raised voice of the commander and listens as he uses his hands to describe the dramatic twists and turns of the aerial combat he has just witnessed. The Grenadier will soon go back over the mist covered fields, to the trenches built during the night.

The tank crew wears the new padded camouflage uniforms delivered to the division at the start of the offensive (Operation Frühlingserwachen). They were somewhat taken aback as to why they did not receive these during the Ardennes offensive in December 1944, when the weather was much colder. The still, dawn

over Papkeszi is cold, but soon the sun will rise to warm the day.

On this day, 9.SS .Pz.Div Hohenstaufen faced their last large battle as a division, and was dug in from Vilonya to Berhida, together with troops from 4.Kav.Div and a Hungarian battle formation. Their task was to hold back the Soviet troops as long as possible, enabling Axis divisions to break through the cauldron at Jenö, where thousands of Waffen SS and Wehrmacht soldiers stood ready to march. "Ausbruch von Jenö Kessel!"

The coming day and night would become horrendous with intense battles involving hand to hand combat and tank duels. Panther 'AJ 9' would finally be blown up by its crew close to the village of Vilonya, when the Russian forces threatened to break through at several places during the next few days: The 5th Guard Tank Corps stood ready to strike with the full force of its tank brigades.

Time for a diorama

In the beginning of my tank modeling career, I exclusively built dioramas and vignettes. I made house ruins and walls from sheets of plaster (drywall), and created historical themes around subjects like a Tiger I in Normandy, a Panther in the Ardennes, an SU-85 in Budapest, or a Jagdpanther in Hungarian Pusztan 1945. These dioramas are long since gone, and unfortunately, only a few were ever photographed. Some were sold and some were displayed in competitions, but eventually I put modelling on the shelf for a couple of years to fully

concentrate on literature and research.

When I returned to modelling, my ambition no longer resided in time consuming dioramas or vignettes, instead I focused on a tank models with figures on a simple wooden base, which is what I did in the following years.

This situation evolved into a struggle between research and model building; was there a way to combine both? My solution to this was that because the research took so much time, the construction of the model became a kind of narrative that I 'wrote', which I believe I have managed successfully. Still, I missed the creative process in constructing dioramas and vignettes, so after a long break, I was finally back where it all started.

The House

The original idea was to build the Panther I had been researching; AJ 9 in Hungary, March 1945; but was I to put it on a wooden base as usual, or in a genuine Hungarian environment? As I have been travelling a lot in the Hungarian countryside, with its wonderful little villages, I felt that I needed to create something more than just the Panther on a simple wooden base. I began drawing sketches of different ideas; I definitely wanted to incorporate a house or part of one typical for the era and location. I opted to have a section of a house with an open door to some sort of garage housing a Schwimmwagen.

During my travels in Hungary; I

have photographed many houses in the countryside, I wanted to capture their character and surrounding atmosphere. From bookshops and antique bookstores in Budapest, I collected books describing traditional house construction with emphasis on rural Hungarian architectural history.

During the construction, I had lots of help and support from my friend Otto Jozsa, who was working at the Limes Models company together with the owners Robert Racz and Geza Csizmazia. They are commercially model makers producing small scale house models for the building industry and have an excellent knowledge of old Hungarian architecture. Otto knew exactly what I was after when I asked him about windows and doors for my project. They were able to laser cut wooden windows and doors, and tiles from styrene plastic that were made to a very high standard. I had decided to make the walls from plaster sheets and after a long and very interesting process; I managed to get the result I had been striving for.

The garage doors are scratch built from wood and I weathered them to show an old and worn look. Drain pipes was

made from aluminium tubing and when the construction phase was completed, I painted and weathered the building with appropriate colours.

The Panther

I used a Dragon Panther as a basis for my model as it is the most accurate on the market. I then used photo etched sets from Aber and Voygager, together with lots of scratch building; like the cleaning rod tube and other smaller details. As I usually do, I lowered the chassis to give the vehicle heavy look and Roddy MacDougall built the reinforced mantle. Roddy was very supportive throughout the construction and painting of the model, and his knowledge of the Panther is impressive.

Roddy managed to get Archer Transfers to produce the turret number 'AJ 9', along with a logical manufacturer's number. The white "A" for the gun travel lock was included in the sheet, what this "A" stood for is still unknown, but we know that it was present on the tanks produced by the M.A.N factory.

As 'AJ 9' was a command version of the Panther (only assembled by M.A.N), I

The Schwimmwagen was updated with PE parts and wider tyres from Sinsengummi.

This rear view clearly shows the star antenna mount on the Befehlspanther. All Befehlspanthers were manufactured at the M.A.N plant and were painted with the appropriate factory applied camouflage scheme from September 1944 to the end of the war.

The highly detailed tracks come from WWII Productions. Note the bare metal finish on the inner wheels, caused by the friction against the guide horns on the tracks.

Note the overlapping schurtzen which are not fitted in the same sequence as when they were painted showing the yellow base coat where the camouflage was not applied.

wanted to include the three extension rods for the FuG8 radio used to enhance its range which I made from brass. I also used the antenna set from Tasca that includes a photo etched star antenna and good quality antenna mounts. The remaining antennas were scratch built from plastic rods that can be shaped to the correct conical profile. This feature was missing from the commercial products available at the time. I found that these products did not have the correct conical shape, were too thick or did not have a sharp enough point. Nowadays several companies' produces brass antennas that looks the part, but often lacks the pointed tip in the correct scale thickness. The tracks I used are from the eminent WW II Productions. As has happened so often before; Dragon released a Befehlspanther just as I finished my build!

The VW Schwimmwagen is the Tamiya offering, updated with an ABER photo etched set and wider wheels from Sinsengumi.

Painting and weathering

9.SS .Pz.Div Hohenstaufen received a delivery Panthers in November 1944 and a few more at the beginning of December. After studying pictures of 'AJ 9' and several other Panthers produced by M.A.N during this timeframe, I painted mine accordingly. For instance, one typical detail for MAN

The old woman looking out of the window is a converted Preiser figure. The window frames were custom made by Limes Models of Hungary.

The battle scarred house was made using plasterboard sheets, this material made it easy to create cracks and bullet holes. The number 3/24 stands for 3.Schw.Pz.Rgt 24 (I./24) - another reminder of the battles during operation Konrad III during January 1945.

AJ79

Panthers is the yellow muzzle break. Once again, Roddy MacDougall acted as mentor and source for the correct M.A.N paint scheme for this period.

I used a cream yellow base, followed by the green camouflage and finally the red brown; all the paints were mixed from the Humbrol range to get as close match as possible to the correct colours. After this, I applied washes and dry brushing to tone down the colours to my liking. The dirt on the wheels was created from fine sand applied before painting which was then weathered with pastel pigments and washes of Humbrol paints.

Figures

I used figures from Alpine, Wolf, Corpus, Gunnar Jansson Production and I had one figure sculpted by Roddy MacDougall according to my specifications. The old woman is from Preiser. The geese are from Tamiya by courtesy of Brian Murdoch and the horse cart was assembled from parts of different kits. All the figures were converted to fit into the scene and they were painted with Humbrol enamels and oils.

Aknowledgement

During the year it took me to build this diorama; the tips, tricks, support and constructive criticism from fellow modellers and friends has been invaluable. Many thanks go to:

Roddy MacDougall
Otto Jozsa and Limes Models, Budapest
Peti Barnaky
Gergö Szaszko
Manus Gallagher
Istvan Toth
Hilary Doyle
Oliver van Hettinga
Edi Eberl
All my friends and colleagues at the "Kampfgruppe" Militaria Internet forum.

Mirko Bayerl

KAUFMANN'S

Using his knowledge of the battle of the Ardennes, Roddy MacDougall has portrayed a vehicle from the spearhead of the German offensive at Stoumont on December 19th 1944. Original photos of Panther 211 served as a guide through out the project.

The Sdkfz 171 Panther and in particular those equipped with the steel tyred road wheels have fascinated me for many years now. The many changes to these vehicles, either brought about by a need to improve production efficiency or as a direct result of combat experience and the speed with which these changes were implemented is impressive. These changes can be used to trace the assembly plant and date that the vehicle was manufactured and constantly reveal new information about this series of vehicles.

The German units chosen to participate in the Ardennes offensive had for the most part been involved in prolonged combat that had resulted in the loss of most of their armoured vehicles. This necessitated that these units were almost entirely re equipped for the forthcoming offensive with new equipment.

One of the spearhead units in this offensive was Kampfgruppe Peiper made up of elements of the Leibstandarte Division, it is one of this units Panthers that I have chosen as the subject of this project.

Panther 211 was the mount of Untersturmfuhrer Hubert Kaufmann, the leader of 1st Platoon, 2nd Company, SS Panzer Regiment 1 of the Leibstandarte SS Adolf Hitler Division. This was one of a trio of Panther that marked the furthest penetration west by KG Peiper. This Panther was knocked out a few hundred metres West of Stoumont Railway station on the 19th December 1944 and several photographs were subsequently taken of this vehicle after it was pushed onto the verge to clear the road.

The model

I had previously built a model of this vehicle in 2004 with steel tyred road wheels, as one

Panther 211 had the Fgst number 121047 stencilled in the middle of the glacis plate. All of the markings are Archer dry transfers; these were chipped and worn to replicate the wear seen in contemporary photos of this vehicle.

Technical drawings courtesy of Panzertracts

STEED

SS Pz. Rgt 1, Stoumont, 19th December 1944

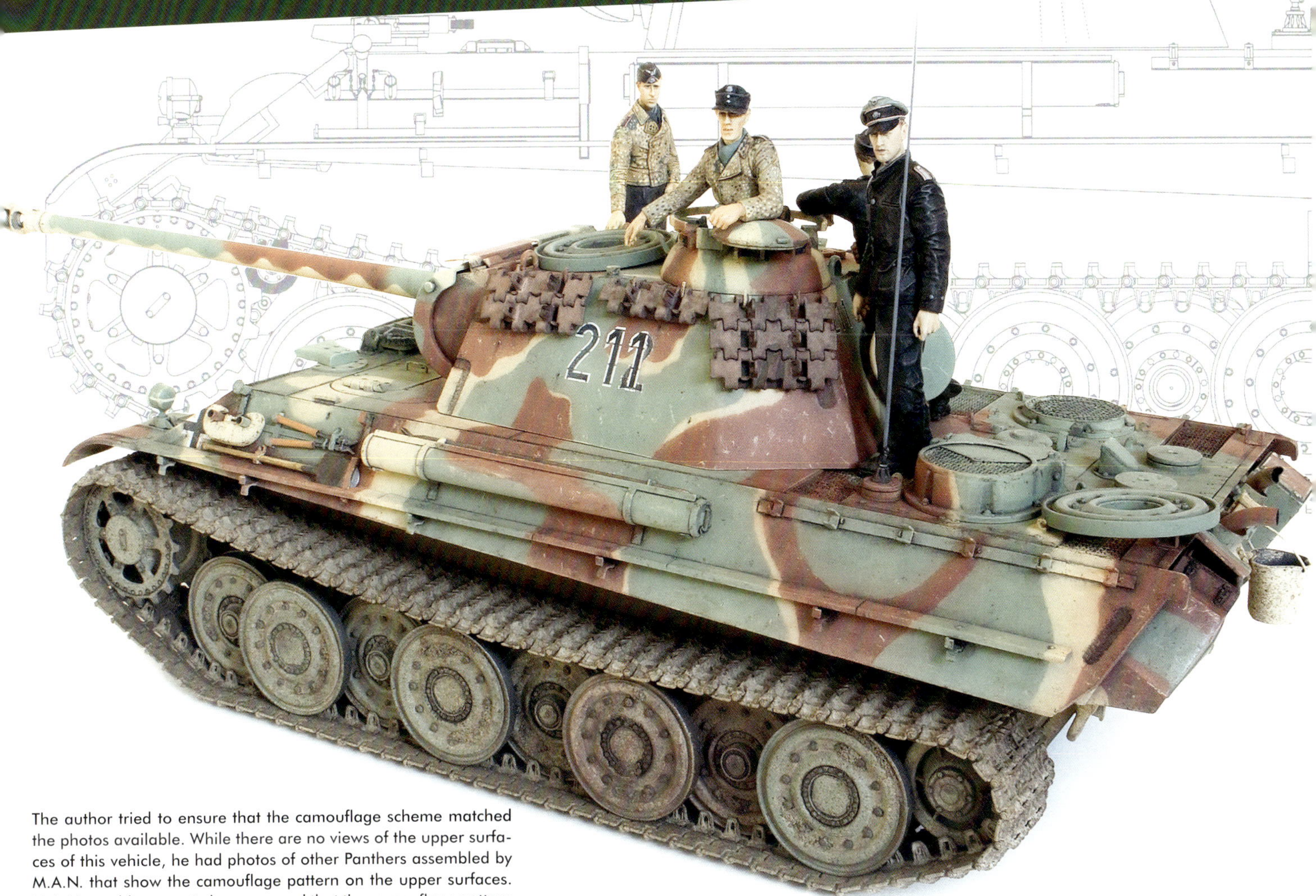

The author tried to ensure that the camouflage scheme matched the photos available. While there are no views of the upper surfaces of this vehicle, he had photos of other Panthers assembled by M.A.N. that show the camouflage pattern on the upper surfaces. M.A.N. would appear to have ensured that the camouflage pattern carried on underneath the edges of the turret on at least some of the Panthers that were assembled after September 1944.

of those involved in the "Duel In The Mist" book project I had access to stills from the cine film taken on the 19th December 1944 by German combat photographers. I had identified what I thought was a spare steel wheel on the engine deck of Panther 211, as it advanced through Stoumont. As none of the locals had subsequently liberated the wheels from the Panther I deduce that it was one of the short run of vehicles assembled by M.A.N. in September 1944, equipped with these wheels. None of the photographs available at that time either confirmed or disproved this theory. Just prior to the publication of "Duel In The Mist" in 2007 two new photographs were discovered that seemed to indicate that this Panther was fitted with the standard rubber tyred road wheels and I amended the captions and artwork in "Duel In The Mist" to reflect this. Inevitably, almost as soon as "Duel In The Mist" was published, we were able to find several new photographs of Panther 211 including several views of the vehicles left hand side. I was able to use these photographs to build as accurate a model of this vehicle as possible with the exception of the side skirts as no photos have surfaced showing the camouflage pattern on these.

The question of which kit used for this project was a very easy choice to make. I would use one of Dragon Models new "smart kit" Panther series, this is an excellent range and for those interested in accuracy they are easily the best on the market. I was able to provide some advice to Dragon Models as they prepared to introduced a dedicated Steel wheeled Panther version (kit 6370) which is the first 1/35 scale kit with correctly dimensioned and detailed steel wheels. There are also several other details such as the MG Kugelblende casting

DML KIT 6370

Some of the changes and additions to the standard kit can be seen in this view of the unpainted model. The armour plate texture applied using the technique pioneered by Makoto Takaishi. The figures are all sculpted using Magic Sculpt over styrene formers, the heads and hands are all Alpine products. The Radio Antenna is a styrene rod shaved to the correct profile, Mirko Bayerl displayed the technique which provides a very slender and accurately profiled antenna in around ten minutes.

variation that was used on the majority of the steel wheeled Panthers included in this kit, which for anyone building one of these vehicles is the only real game in town.

I prefer to work with either styrene or resin and as I intended to build several of Panthers using the Dragon kit as a base, I worked on a set of master parts that could be used to reduce the work involved in rectifying the limitations of injection moulding styrene on very small and thin parts.

Small parts such as the spare track brackets, schurtzen hooks and the vehicles tool brackets are very difficult to mold to scale thickness, the parts provided in the kit are really quite good but are still not at the correct scale thickness. I made a new set of parts to overcome the question of scale thickness and to provide enhanced detail for things like the jack block and bracket, gun travel lock, spare track changing cable etc' which Accurate Armour cast in resin and now market as accessory set A116 which I would use on this build.

I rework the fenders and side rails first as these involve the most work and are the areas where the most care is needed. I have developed a technique for reworking styrene to represent damaged sheet metal components that involves thinning the styrene using a motor tool with a combination of milling bits and sanding drums. I carefully shave the hidden surfaces of the parts, the inner face of the rear stowage boxes or the lower surface of the fenders to a point where I can easily see daylight through them (approx .5-1 mm thick). This requires a little practice and I have ruined more than a couple of kits with over enthusiasm, you need to do this slowly and in steps so that heat does not build up in the part to the extent that it starts to melt or deform as this will be very difficult to rectify later. When the part is suitably thin place the face that will be exposed on the finished model on top of a firm rubber surface that will support the part but not crush any fine surface detail such as strengthening ribs, hinges or rivets. Using a burnishing tool create pressure on the inner face of the styrene so that it becomes stressed and starts to turn a lighter shade of grey, again care need to be taken here as too much pressure will cause the tool to split the styrene. When the styrene has turned light grey the part can now be carefully bent to shape to match damage seen in photographs with the possibility to replicate very extreme levels of damage. If the finished face of the styrene starts to split, fill this with a small amount of cyanoacrylate glue to stop the split travelling as you continue to work the part. The excess glue can easily be cleaned up with fine wet and dry paper when you have finished reworking the part. When this was done, I added texture to the armour plate using the stippled primer technique pioneered by the Japanese modeller Makoto Takaishi. The rest of the hull assembly was quite strait forward, essentially following the assembly sequences laid out in the kit instructions with a few minor alterations as I had made new tool brackets from sheet styrene to allow for scale thickness. I made an antenna out of shaved styrene rod and used some custom etched parts for the engine grills and jack bracket along with a beautifully turned ring for the crew compartment heater that I was sent by Gunnar Jansson. These parts are the best brass photo etched parts that I have seen and are greatly enhance the detail on the model.

The turret armour was textured using the stippled primer technique and I reworked the weld seems around the front plate/trunnion armour casting to match the photos of Panther 211. The joint on the trunnion armour were very carefully filled and faired in with particular attention being paid to the joint on the left hand side, this part is a one piece casting and should look like it. I also added the casting lug detail to the centre point of the trunnion side and textured the part to represent an armour casting. The mantle debris guard was thinned at the edges to represent sheet metal and new pilze were turned on a Como drill from styrene rod. I also turned a new rain guard from styrene rod to enhance the detail on the mantle itself. I replaced the brace on the rear turret lifting point with sheet styrene and thinned the periscope guards on the cupola a little. I textured the cupola to represent a casting and added the small lug to the top of the commanders hatch bracket seen on

The rear stowage bin, sheet metal exhaust shrouds and the starboard exhaust pipe were all reworked from the kits styrene parts to replicate damage visible on Panther 211 in the cine film taken in Stoumont on the 19th December 1944.

some but not all Panther Ausf G's. Amongst the last items added were photo etched gas detector panel mounts and a commander's cupola sighting vane again courtesy of Gunnar Jansson. I added the distinctive spare track hooks mounted on the upper edge of the turret on most of Kampfgruppe Peiper's Panthers. These were made with plastic sheathed garden tie wire and glued in place with cayano'.

The figures

I now needed to start making decisions about what figures I would include as the level of detail that would be visible around any open hatches had to be considered. I had a scene in mind based loosely around a photo of Panthers from the 9th Panzer division taken during the opening phase of the Ardennes offensive that showed most of the crew outside the vehicle as they stopped during a pause in the advance. I had initially considered using stock Alpine figures, these are the best currently available on the market, interact well with each other and are a mini vignette in a box. However, I wanted my Panther crew to interact with the vehicle as well as each other; this would necessitate rebuilding or scratch building figures to try to emulate the scene I had in mind. The majority of Kampfgruppe Peiper's tank crews wore the two piece black leather U-boat suit, as it was warm, comfortable and provided a degree of protection from fire.

I first made styrene armatures made from suitable torso's and legs from my spares box ground to shape using my Como drill and sanding drums. There is a fair amount of trial and error at this stage but as the clothing will all be ground of and replaced, the inevitable slips are not too critical. I used styrene rod for the arms as this allows much more scope for adjustment and Taesung Harmms the owner of Alpine Miniatures very kindly provided a variety of heads etc' from his range for both this project and Mirko Bayerl's Panther crew. When I was happy with the anatomy, I then started to cloth the figures using Magic-Sculpt, paying careful attention to references in order to try to capture the look of the uniforms. I use a

The weathering was very restrained in order to show the camouflage scheme more clearly.

The figures were all painted using acrylics, this was the first time that the author had used this medium which requires a different technique to the enamels that he would normally use.

variety of Royal Sovereign silicone rubber paint pushers for sculpting the majority of the clothing folds and some needles of different diameters for the sharper folds.

As the loader would be seated on the turret rear escape hatch and a fair amount of the internal detail from this hatch would be visible I decided to use the M.A. Mori part for this. I had made the master for the escape hatch for M.A. Mori along with several other Panther parts a few years ago, this was designed to fit the Tamiya Panther Ausf G but with a little adjustment to the hinge it could also be used on the Dragon kit.

Painting

With the construction mostly completed, it was now time to start planning the paint. This was quite a daunting prospect as it was more than five years since I had last painted a model other than undercoating it to check for flaws. I have always used Humbrol enamels as I am familiar with their properties and they are relatively easy to come by. They are extremely tough and hard wearing paints with a wide variety of colours. However, they are also unforgiving of any airbrush set up that has the pressure set too high or if they are not mixed and thinned using Humbrol's own thinners. I had to relearn this lesson the hard way and ended up stripping the Panther a few times as I struggled to get a nice smooth coat of paint. I prefer to work from light to dark so always start of with an overall coat of Dunkelgelb, which in this instance was Humbrol 148. I think this light creamy tan colour is a very good match for factory fresh Dunkelgelb. When this had cured for a couple of days, I then start to carefully map out the colour fields of Rot Braun and Olive Grun over this using children's water colour pens. I had previously used expensive artists water colour pens for this until I realised that children's pens worked equally as well and are considerably cheaper. Using a water colour allows the pattern to be easily adjusted to match reference photos as any changes are easily made using water to clean the colour from the surface of the enamel without leaving any residue, it is easier to get the pattern right at this stage rather than discover an error after applying enamels or acrylics. Once I was happy with the colour fields, I used a very heavily thinned coat of enamel applied with a brush to mark the colour fields. I do this so that when I start to lay in the main colours using the airbrush, I only need to concentrate on following the edges and keeping the spray pattern tight. This is easier than trying to match a colour field accurately from photos at the same time as keeping nice tight edges to the colour fields. Any water colour residue can easily be washed off with water and a little soap once the enamel has cured completely.

When this had all fully cured the decals were applied using Archer Transfers set AR35199, these were then dry brushed and washed to lift out the detail and textures that had been applied. This was done using the basic camouflage colours lightened with Humbrol 103 and 148 in varying degrees, the washes were heavily thinned Humbrol matt black. I used a mixture of brown and grey for the chipping which I tried to keep subtle so that it is not immediately apparent and can only be seen on closer inspection. I decided to keep the weathering restrained on this model to leave most of the camouflage pattern clearly visible, only the wheels and rear hull have had a heavier application of drying mud and spattering from the road march.

I used WWII production tracks as they are articulated when assembled and have a nice catenary curve when installed. They are easier to assemble than Model Kasten tracks but have a fair amount of air bubbles and flash that needs to be taken care of. These were base coated in Tamiya acrylic buff and then weathered with enamels and graphite from a Berol artist's pencil.

The figures were my first serious foray in using acrylics to paint uniforms and flesh tones. The rapid drying time of this medium is a mixed blessing, several coats can be applied very quickly but there isn't much room for error as the paint dries too rapidly to go back and remove any excess that has been applied. One of the upsides of acrylics is that they are very easily stripped so that if you are not happy, it is quick and easy to start again without damaging the figure. I was given some very good advice on how to tackle the erbsenmuster camouflage pattern by Calvin Tan, he sent me some very high resolution photos which helped tremendously when I was trying to shade and highlight this complicated pattern. I used Archer transfers for the shoulder boards but chose to paint the exquisitely sculpted detail on the Alpine resin heads which completed the figures.

I must mention Hilary Doyle who allowed us to use his drawing and provided technical advice. I would also like to thank Mirko Bayerl, Manus Gallagher, Darren Gawle and Brian Murdoch for their help and support as well as Taesung Harmms of Alpine Miniatures and Gunnar Jansson without whose help the detail on this project would not be what it is.

Roddy MacDougall

The ubiquitous bucket that no German AFV from World War II should be without is a reworked Tamiya bucket from their Sdkfz 251 kit.

One of the distinctive attributes to the factory applied camouflage schemes on Panthers assembled by M.A.N. is the tightly sprayed edges to the colour fields, it should be loose enough to have been obviously applied with a spray gun, but tight enough that the colour fields are distinct from each other.

The tactical number painted on the turrets port side was originally 212, which was then changed to 211. The tactical numbers on the starboard and rear side have not been changed which suggest either a mistake by the Werkstatt or a change in the vehicles designated commander that was not communicated to the Werkstatt.

RETREAT FROM ANZIO

The editor took on a modelling project that had been on his mind for many years, inspired by a well known photo of Panther 114 of I./Pz. Rgt.4, taken in the Anzio area in 1944.

On January 22nd 1944 the Allies launched operation Shingle, a large amphibious landing at Anzio, just South of Italy's capital Rome. The purpose of this landing was to out flank the German lines in the Cassino area and by doing so, break the stalemate at the German Gustav Line. The Germans were taken completely by surprise and the Allied Task Force met very light resistance. They were able to establish a firm beachhead. By the end of the first day of the operation, 36.000 troops and over 3000 vehicles had been put ashore.

The German commander in Italy, Albert Kesselring was informed of the Allied landing early in the morning and immediately ordered the 4. Fallshirmjäger division, which was undergoing a refit near Rome, to set up defensive positions along all roads leading to Rome. The same order was given to the replacement units from the Panzer Division Hermann Göring, also stationed near Rome.

To set up a defensive perimeter around Anzio, Kesselring sent the following units to the area 1. Fallshirmjäger Korps including the 3 Pz.gren. Rgt., the 71. Infanteri division, elements of Pz. Div. Hermann Göring. The 26. Pz. Div. and the 1. Fallshirmjäger div. were also ordered to send what they could to Anzio. The Wehrmacht high command (OKW) also ordered a number of reinforcements to be sent to Italy. Among these were the I./Pz. Rgt 4, stationed in France, then undergoing training with the new Panther tank.

Surprisingly, the commander of the Allied operation, General Lucas did not take the opportunity to move inland from the beachhead and secure vital junctions while the German presence in the area was still weak. Instead, the build up continued

and a week after the first landings over 60.000 Allied troops had landed ready for a major offensive. However, by that time the Germans had managed to transport over 70.000 troops to the Anzio area.

After the first week of small but intensive assaults the Allies launched their first major offensive from the beachhead on January 29th. It soon became clear that this would not be an easy game, the offensive met stiff resistance and ground to a halt. The Germans launched several counter attacks between the 3 and 11th and the battle raged back and forth. The first major counter attack, Operation Fishfang, was launched on February 16th. This Operation's aim was to split the Allied beachhead in two. For four days, the Germans attacked ferociously with the biggest force used by the Germans during the 1944, apart from the Ardennes offensive. Although it caused severe damage to the Allied forces, the Germans did not succeed in breaking the Allied defences.
Operation Fishfang cost the Germans over 5000 dead, and the Allies 3.500 dead. Both sides were exhausted after the intense fighting and the constant artillery shelling, ironically the operation aimed to break the Cassino stalemate was now in a stalemate itself. The battle in the Anzio area was dominated by artillery fire due to the flat nature of the landscape and this was soon reminiscent of the WWI artillery barrages. With both sides severely beaten up, neither side had the strength or resources to make any serious further attempt to break the stalemate. Smaller encounters and heavy shelling dominated March and April.

Operation Buffalo

By mid May, the Allies starts operation Diadem in order to finally take Monte

Cassino, which they managed to do on May 17th. At the same time, the forces at Anzio prepared for a major break out from the beachhead and on May 23 Operation Buffalo was launched. This focused on the Velletri gap and the Alban hills and from there the access to Highway 6 leading to Rome. Although the advance met resistance and had to run through large minefields, the first days objectives were accomplished. Highway 7 was reached near Cisterna, which was taken on May 25th after two days of intensive fighting. The siege of Anzio was finally over.

Panther deployment

Following the allied landings at Anzio, the I./Pz. Rgt 4 , which was the only Panther unit to be deployed in Italy, was ordered to transfer from France to Italy where it arrived on January 30th. The battalion undertook a road march that lasted several days before reaching their destination. There were numerous mechanical breakdowns on this march. During February, the battalion sporadically participated in the battle in the Anzio area but did not make any significant impact. Many of the Panther suffered from mechanical problems caused by the long road march earlier and did not even reach the combat zone. The bad weather also made the terrain muddy which further decreased their mobility.

After the German counter attacks in the Anzio area failed, the battalion was withdrawn from the front and sent to Prattica di Mare were it was held in reserve. Much needed maintenance and training took place here until May. The combat strength was 64 from the 70 Panthers by May 1st as many had returned from maintenance during the past month and not many had been lost in combat in February, but rather due to mechanical problems an thus been able to be recovered.

Following the Allied offensives in the Cassino and Anzio area the battalion was put on alert and was initially put under the command of the LI. Gebirgsjäger corps. They were sent to support the 715 Inf. Div. and on the 19th of May they were located just east of Velletri, behind the 715. Inf.Div.

Early on May 20th the battalion began a road march to the Frosinone area some 50 km to the east, where it was subordinated to the 26. Pz.Div. From May 21st onwards the battalion was in action some 30 km southeast of Frosinone, in the area of Pico and Ceprano where it stayed until May 28. During the fighting in this area the 4. Kompanie claimed 33 tank victories.

The photo of Panther 114 however,

The original photo of 114 taken in Torre Tre Ponti on May 25th 1944. Note the zimmerit coating on the loose schürzen. Traces of camouflage over the Dunkelgelb can be seen on the front glacis, around the Balkenkreuz and on the cleaning rod tube.

NARA via Panzerwrecks

UPDATES OF THE KIT

1. Aber barrel.
2. Vyager Models fenders, brackets, toolholders etc.
3. Aber side skirts.
4. Turned brass lids, courtesy of Gunnar Jansson.
5. Tube for cleaning rods made from lead foil.
6. Artisan Mori cupola.
7. Zimmerit from Cavallier

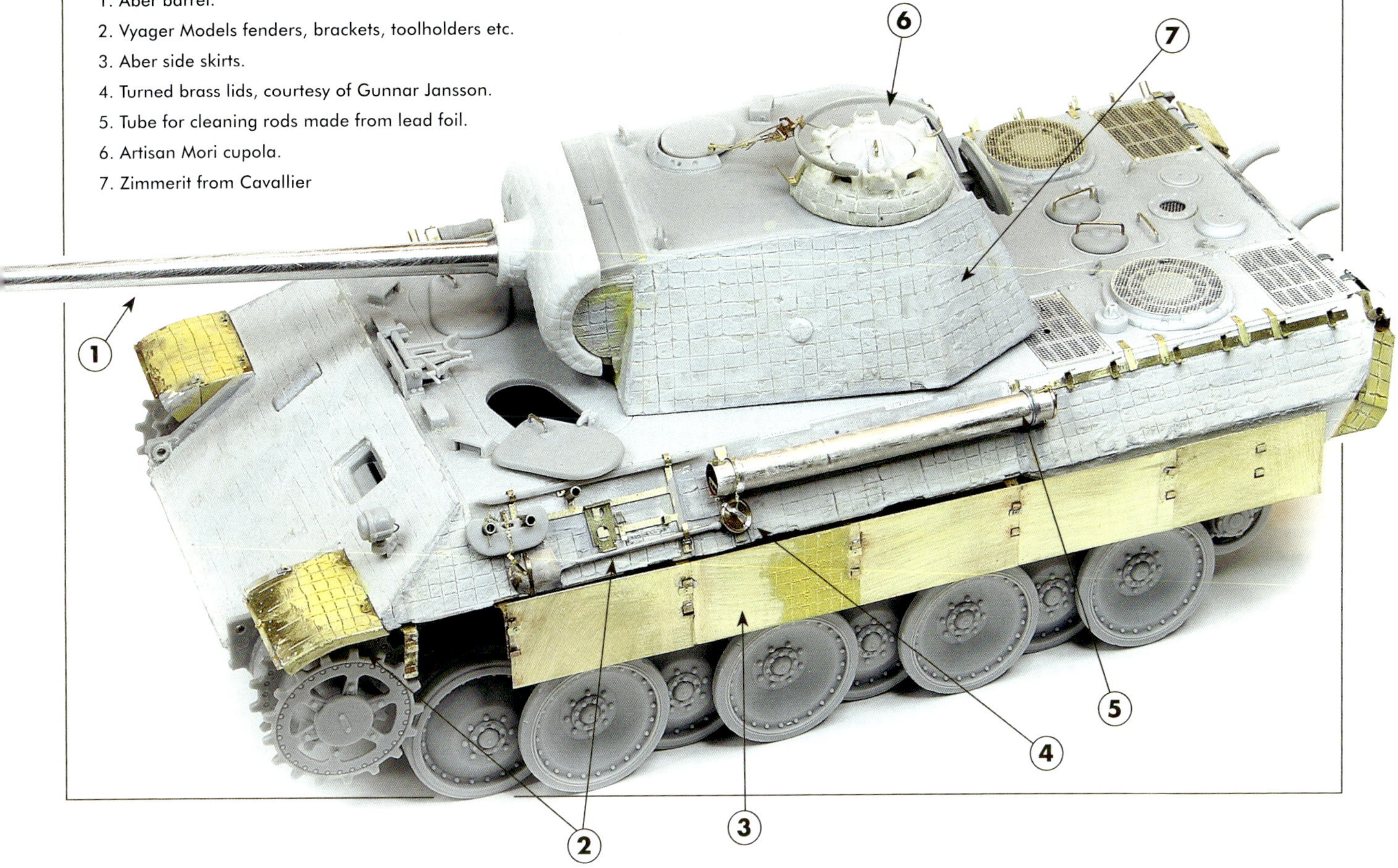

DML KIT 6160

was taken at Torre Tre Ponti, some 60 km west of the 1. Kompanie´s location. So what was it doing there? According to the combat reports, the battalion lost many of it's Panthers on the road march to the Frosonone area, on the evening of the 20th May only 19 of the 70 Panthers had reached Frosinone. Panther 114 was probably left behind due to mechanical problems, when the US VI Corps broke out of Anzio and reached Via Appia on the 23rd of May it had not been recovered. The recovery crews were extremely busy and were not able to reach all of the vehicles that had broken down. The damage on the Panther indicates that it was blown up buy its crew rather than being knocked out.

Construction

Panther 114 was likely to have been assembled some time between late September and late October 1943. This can be determined by the external features such as the MG ring mount on the cupola, this was not introduced until mid September 1943. The MG port on the front glacis is the letterbox type and not the later Kugelblende which was introduced in November 1943. The gun sight is still the binocular sight, this was replaced by a monocular sight in November. There are other features that indicate the vehicle was assembled within the October/November timeframe such as the exhaust pipes and the horizontal jack stowage on the rear hull plate.

I used Dragon's Panther Ausf A, Early model, which was released in 2002 and was the first of several Panther kits released by this company. It suitably represents the September/October production vehicle that I needed for this project. The kit does not have the articulated suspension that the newer Panther kits have and there no extras such as photo etch etc' included. However, it is still a very good kit, but as always there was room for improvement.

First of all an appropriate zimmerit coating had to be applied to the vertical armour surfaces. I was not sure if I would have a go at making my own coating from putty, or if I would use a resin set. After examining the commercially available sets I decided to use Cavalier's and use putty to fill in the gaps and cover sections missing in the cavalier set. The resin zimmerit was carefully cut out, test fitted, and to my surprise there was not too much re shaping needed. The trickiest parts were cutting out the areas where the tool holders would later be fitted and to make all the edges meet without any major gaps. Some filling and patching was required after the resin sheets were fixed in place and this was done using Tamiya epoxy putty and Magic Sculpt. All of the zimmerit coating on the rear hull plate, rear stowage boxes and front fenders was made from Tamiya putty, which I stippled with a sponge to get the right texture.

Once the zimmerit was fixed in place, I proceeded with the basic build, which was rather straight forward. I decided to add some weld seams around the periscope guards and along the upper turret edges. To enhance some of the details on the model, I incorporated Voyager Model's Panther A/D set, which is extensive and includes all the tool holders, fenders, grills, MG mount, rails for the spare tracks etc'. I used an Aber barrel and schurzen as well as a Tiger models detail set for the escape hatch. The tube for the gun cleaning rods was made from lead foil and my friend Gunnar Jansson provided me two brass lids he had turned on a lathe which were a joy to add. One thing I discovered when studying the photo of 114 was that one of the schurzen carried a zimmerit coating, so I applied a thin layer of Tamiya putty and textured this appropriately. The schurzen sections and brackets were then soldered together for better strength and stability and fitted to the model.

One of the few weak spots on this DML kit is the turret cupola, which lacks periscopes some and other details. Fortunately, Modelling Artisan Mori offers an excellent upgraded cupola that includes periscopes, hatch and the hatch pivoting mechanism fitted to the inside of the cupola. I applied a zimmerit coating to the cupola before installing it in the turret.

Painting

With the assembly largely complete, it was time for the painting process. At first this seemed to be a straightforward procedure, painting a plain yellow tank cannot be that hard I thought. My only concern was how to weather the zimmerit areas. Just prior to painting the model, I examined the photo of 114 and discovered traces of what could be camouflage paint over the dunkelgelb. It's funny, because it seems that everyone who models an Italian theatre Panther Ausf A, takes for granted that all of them were plain dunkelgelb and I was about to make the same mistake! Determining colours in a black and white photo is always difficult, especially so if the tank was photographed in bright sunlight and covered in dust. But after consulting Roddy MacDougall and a few other Panther experts, I was at least 80% sure that the darker areas on the tank was camouflage and not just soot as I had first thought. When comparing the sooty areas that could be determined by obvious fire damage, with the camouflaged areas they were clearly different in appearance.

I gave the model a coat of Games Workshop Chaos Black, which works well

as primer, giving a semi gloss finish. I then mixed the dunkelgelb base coat from Tamiya acrylics, starting with a rather dark version of dunkelgelb. This was subsequently followed by a couple of light coats, which created an illusion of depth on the surface. I moved on to the camouflage colours, which I applied in a random pattern, trying to imitate the pattern I could see in the photo of 114.

With the three colour camouflage scheme in place, I gave the entire model a thin coat of Johnson's clear floor polish. This gives a strong barrier that will provide protection to the paint during the weathering process. The model looks very much like a toy at this stage but that would soon change.

I gave the model a couple of thin dark brown oil washes, which immediately bring out the details and recesses on the model. To further accentuate this effect, a more concentrated wash was applied around the smaller surface details and the deepest recesses. When the washes had dried for a day, I went applied the chipping and scratches, using mainly Vallejo acrylics. I started with a couple of yellow tones and made subtle scratches and chips to bring the surface to life. This was made both by using a brush but also with a sponge on some of the larger areas. The effect is subtle and barely visible but is a huge improvement when compared to a plain dunkelgelb surface. I also simulated areas of chipped off camouflage colour by adding the yellow chips on to some of the green and brown camouflage.

To give the model a worn look, I also applied grey chipping to simulate bare metal. This is easily overdone, so the procedure must be done slowly and examined after each step to ensure that it is not overdone. I used Vallejo acrylics for this as well as one of my favourite mixes, black oil and printer's ink silver. This mix looks a bit greasy and is ideal for areas where it is likely that oil has been used to lubricate hinges etc. I used this mix mainly on the towing clevises and the towing shackles.

One of the trickiest parts of the painting was to bring the zimmerit surface to life, even if the washes helped a great deal. Factory zimmerit could vary from light greyish to yellowish, and I decided to simulate the worn zimmerit areas by making subtle grey chipping to make it look like exposed zimmerit. The areas where the zimmerit had come of completely I used a red brown colour to simulate the primer colour underneath the coating. Again, this is an effect that can easily be overdone so I kept it very subtle.

Final assembly

With the painting and chipping done, it

This side view clearly shows the partial zimmerit coating on the schürzen, with the red primer showing on the worn areas.

was time to add the tow cables, tracks and the final details. I used Friul Model tracks which were painted dark brown then heavily washed with a mixture of Humbrols, oils and a small amount of Vallejo pigments. This mix gradually built up a layer that looks like dried mud and dust. I then gave the tracks a light dry brush with dark grey oils followed by graphite to bring back some of the metallic shine.

The tow cables are a mix of Karaya wire and SKP Model cable eyes. The cable was bent into the desired shape before being painted dark grey, it was then dry brushed with the oil/silver mixture to give it a slight sheen. I attached one of the kit's towing clevises to the end of one of the cables to make it look more interesting as I had seen this in a couple of photos. The antenna is a brass item from SKP and fits perfectly in the antenna mount.

One prominent feature in the photo of 114 and other Panthers in Italy are the wooden corduroy mats used to help the tank get a better grip in when stuck in mud. I experimented with both wood and plastic to recreate these. I ended up using plastic rod and sprue, which were given a wooden texture using coarse sanding paper and the tip of a modelling knife. The wooden pieces were then tied together using surgical thread and super glue before being painted in a variety of grey and brown shades using Vallejo colours.

I finished off the painting and weathering by adding some earth tone washes to the running gear, lower hull and lower chassis followed by a thin coat of Model Master matt varnish over the entire model.

The vignette

I always try to display my models on a scenic base as I think it brings the model to life. It gives the viewer a sense of what type environment the vehicle operated in, if it supposed to be winter or summer, dry, wet etc. I also think that the scenery surrounding the model is one of the most enjoyable aspects of modelling, as it really challenges the modeller to be creative. I wanted to depict a semi urban environment and include some buildings, as I am interested in architecture. After studying some reference photos I had taken on a vacation in Italy, I decided to make two buildings connected to each other to create a back drop for the model. I have worked with many different materials when making buildings but I still prefer working with plaster, which I find easy to cast, scribe, shape etc. The lower building was created using a mould I had for many years but had never used. It was originally a 1/48 railroad building but is also suitable for 1/35. I cast three sheets and cut them to fit next to each other, making up three walls. A hole for the door was cut using a fine saw blade. I then went on to the taller building. I took some Evergreen sheets and made a mould with different levels in it to create the area around the window, below the roof and the base of the house. I cast the walls in plaster and cut out the hole for the window before fitting it to the lower building, using epoxy glue and plaster for filling the seams.

The roof sections were Model Victoria's beautifully cast resin roof sheets. They are very well detailed and are the typical Southern European style of roof tile. I painted the roofs in a variety of terra cotta shades and gave them a wash of brown oils.

The small chair was scratchbuild form plastic card/rod and given flaked paint effect.
Note the exhaust outlets, detailed with wire.

To further detail the buildings, I added window shutters from MiniArt. I then scratch built a wall light using plastic eyes originally intended for making eyes on kids toys, a great tip I got from Mike Bishop of Monroe Perdu. The wiring on the wall is lead wire, which is also a very useful material. The doors on the lower building were made from plastic card textured with coarse sand paper. The buildings were painted with Humbrols, Vallejo acrylics and then given various washes with brown oils. I sanded the walls slightly with fine sanding paper to simulate colour faded by the elements.

The commander figure is an Alpine figure that was modified to fit the turret cupola, a radio head set was also added. The radio operator is a Tank figure, more or less out of the box but with an Alpine head. The old woman in the window comes from Plus Model's Refugee set and only needed some minor adjustments to fit. I tried to make the old woman's eyes meet the tank commander's to create some interaction.

I initially intended to have a figure in the driver's hatch but since the Panther A could not be driven if the driver was not in the driver's seat I omitted him, as I wanted to give the impression that the Panther was moving forward.

With the houses painted and weathered I pinned and glued them on the base and started making the groundwork. A mixture of plaster, acrylic colours and fine sand was applied in thin layers. While it was still wet, I pressed small stones, leaves and other

The wall lamp was scratch built and the wiring was made from lead wire. The window shutters are from MiniArt.

debris into it. When it was dry, I painted the groundwork in a variety of earth tones to make it less monotone. As a final touch, I added some grass turfs from Joefix studios as well as some leaves made from dry flowers and dry spices.

Conclusion

This was a very rewarding project that gave me the chance to engulf my self in reference books on the battles in the Anzio area as well as the Panther A. For me, modelling and history have tended to go more hand in hand for each project, and I very seldom make a model "just for fun" nowadays. However, it is still a hobby that I enjoy of course!

I would like to thank Roddy MacDougall and Mirko Bayerl for providing me details about the Panther A, and Martin Block for sharing his tremendous knowledge about the Panthers in Italy. Without their help, this project would have been more difficult to research. I would also like to thank all participants in this book for being a source of inspiration with their own builds.

Finally, I would like to extend my gratitude to Lee Archer for providing me with the photo of Panther 114.

Toni Canfora

References:
Anzio - Beleagured Beachhead by Steve Zaloga
Fatal Decision - Anzio and the battle for Rome by Carlo D´Este
Panzer V Panther by Walter J. Spielberger, Hilary Doyle and Thomas L. Jentz

The roofs on the houses come from the excellent Model Victoria range and has a typical Mediterranean appearance. The telegraph pole was originally a railway accessory but some minor modifications made it suitable for use on a 1/35 military diorama.

PANTHER SCHÜRZEN IN SIMONTORNYA

Mirko carefully examine and document the schürzen found in Simontornya. It probably belonged to a Panther from 1.SS. Pz. Div. LAH.

- and other rarities found in the battlefields today

By Mirko Bayerl

A couple of years ago, I came across a Hungarian Militaria collector, Mr. T, on an Internet forum who had found a Panther schürzen that was still in fairly good condition. It was possible to distinguish the three camouflage colours rot braun, grün and dunkelgelb on it. I was tempted to travel to Hungary again, as I have done so many times before in my research of military history. I wanted to meet Mr. T and have a chance to study the Panther schürzen at first hand.

I contacted Mr. T, by e-mail and after some correspondence I arranged to visit him together with Otto Josza and Peter Barnaky. The journey involved travelling from Budapest to Simontornya, which is a small town, some 50-60kms from Szekesfehervar, where the Schürtzen was found.

At the end of Second World War, the 1.SS Panzer Division Leibstandarte Adolf Hitler (LAH) fought both in and around Simontornya during operation "spring awakening". They lost three or four Panthers during the battle in this area. The division did not advance any further than this before it was forced to retreat following the Russians offensive "Operation Vienna", just north of Szekesfehervar which forced the cancellation of the German attack. The schürtzen probably belong to one of the Panthers that were lost in this area.

Interesting discoveries

There have been many discussions regarding German camouflage colours and the order of their application in 1944-45 over the years. There are many different points of view regarding this subject. Was it a grün base, dunkelgelb or even rot braun, we had brought a scalpel with us and had permission from Mr. T, to scrape away a small section of paint in order to try and ascertain how the colours had been applied.

To our astonishment, we had some rather unexpected results! The paint on the rear or inside face was a very thin, hard, red primer, underneath which was bare metal. Turning to the outer face, it was time to find out what base colour had been used on this particular part. Very carefully, a small area of each of the three camouflage colours was scraped away; we discovered a grey primer applied directly to the bare metal underneath the paint. This was the case underneath two of the camouflage colours, the rot braun and the grün. The dunkelgelb camouflage had been applied over the top of the other two colours on this item. After deliberating this for some time, we concluded that there was no single overall coat of paint applied to the primer on this part! There are many discussions on the Internet that mention this grey paint, it was a zinc phosphate primer used by German industry at this time and after the war. A description of this zinc phosphate primer was given to the author by someone currently employed in the steel industry,

"The zinc phosphate primer was a protective anti-corrosive coating applied to steel plate/sheet while it is stored, by manufacturers and shipyards prior to delivery to the end users, i.e., the vehicle assembly plants. It was meant as a temporary protection from rust."

Mr. Denecke wrote in his book "Tarnanstriche des deutschen Heeres 1914 bis heute", that metal parts were treated with phosphate to inhibit rust.

The grey zinc phosphate primer was not a camouflage paint used due to shortages of other paints, but a layer of protection on which either red oxide primer or the actual camouflage paint could be applied. The rot braun and grün paint was sprayed on in turn, only covering the area that would be exposed in that colour in order to save paint, and finally the dunkelgelb was sprayed on in diagonal stripes.

The paint on the Schürzen was very soft and when scraped off turned to a powder which coloured the fingers if ground. Its application was not even and was thicker in some places; the dunkelgelb however, was very thickly applied. It appeared to have been spitting from the spray gun, staining the rot braun and grün areas, a true nightmare for us modellers!

I would like to thank Peter Barnaky and Otto Josza for their help and support while researching this information.

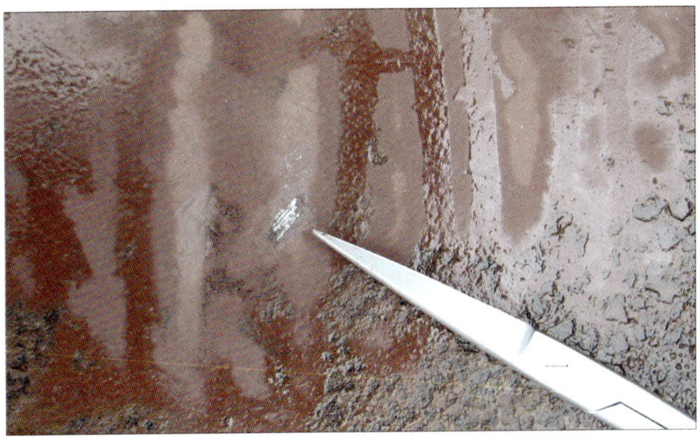

The backside of the schürzen was primer red. When the surface was scraped with a scalpel the bare metal show through.

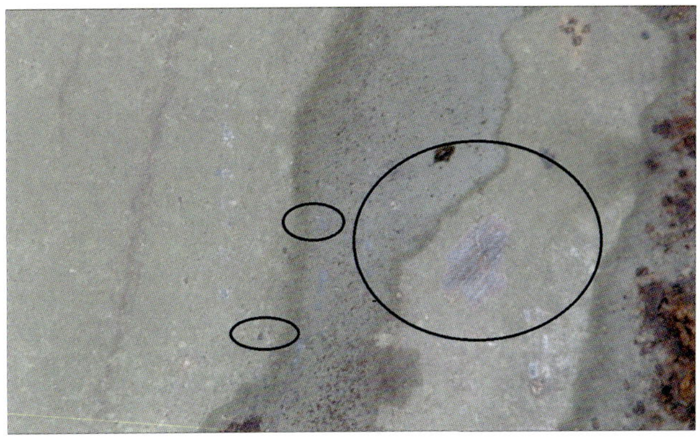

The outside of the schürzen. Surprisinly, when the colour was scraped off, a grey primer appeared.

Note the unsharp edges and the thick consistency of the yellow colour.

Overall view of the schürtzen, clearly showing the three colours; green, red brown, and yellow.

Colour application on the Panther Schürzen found in Simontornya

First, a grey zinc phosphate primer is applied over the bare metal.

The green layer is then applied, but not over the entire schürzen, so no overall coat

The red brown colour then covers the rest of the schürzen, egde to edge with the reen colour,

Finally, thin stripes of yellow is applied. The previous colurs partially still shows through.

Read more about the battlefield findings in Hungary on the next pages...

RARITIES FOUND IN THE BATTLEFIELDS TODAY

This gallery of photos from Hungary has been added as an addition to my other articles in this book. When travelling in the Hungarian countryside to interview people, I have on many occasions noticed the scars of war are still visible in peoples every day lives. Everything from track links, wheels and gun barrels can be found in gardens and on farms. The items have come in handy for the farmers and craftsmen. The pictures that follow in this section were taken on location. Local historians who spend their weekends on the old battlefields were consulted where possible. They go alone or in groups, bringing maps, shovels and sometimes metal detectors to examine old trenches etc. I have participated in several of these field trips and find them both relaxing and exiting. One should be careful of course, as live ammunition can still be found, people who are familiar with such items should always be present. The pictures were taken by Gergö Szaszko, Mirko Bayerl, Zoltan W, and Otto Josza.

Gas mask case and ammunition box found near Lake Balaton, they are in excellent condition given their age and the materials that they were constructed with.

The armoured front plate from an Sdkfz 251. We should note the colour and patina of the metal which does not show any sign of severe rusting or pitting.

It is still possible to find road wheels from a German halftrack being used on a farm cart. The tyres are worn after 6 years but the wheel is still in very good condition.

This set of extended armoured guards came from an Sdkfz 251/9 in the area of Simontornya. The other parts from the vehicle confirm that it was this type of vehicle.

The barrel of a 3.7cm Flak gun was found in a garden, it is still in quite good condition but would never be able to stand the pressure of firing a round through it again!

The towing Clevis from a King Tiger that belonged to s.Pz.Abt. 503, it still shows traces of the original Dunkelgelb paint.

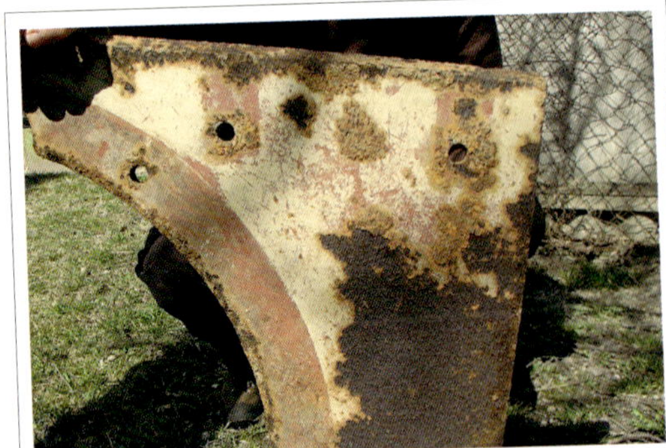

This is the plate that surrounds the air intake fan casting on a Panther Ausf A engine deck. Traces of red primer can be seen along with an application over this of Dunkelgelb paint.

This commanders hatch is from a different Panther to the plate in the previos photo. It also shows quite a large section of the original dunkelgelb paint.

The drivers hatch from a Wiking Panther Ausf A. The hatch is from one of the Panthers photographed in Markus Erikson's article. Note the Dunkelgelb colour and the rubber pad.

The roof of a Tiger II Ausf B that belonged to s.Pz. Abt. 503. The red primer is still particularly evident on this part which is still in very good condition.

The anti grenade screens from the same Tiger II Ausf B, some traces of the original paint are still evident.

The Idler wheel from the same Tiger II Ausf B, there are some traces of Green paint but the majority of the remaining paint is Dunkelgelb that has been stained to a very dark shade when compared to other original items finished in this colour.

The commanders hatch from this Tiger II Ausf B shows the double curvature present on the main surface of the casting. There are large areas of the original paint still visible on this part.

The wheel from this Tiger II Ausf B is in poor condition, however, some Dunkelgelb paint can still be seen on it

The rear door of an Sdkfz 250, the door was found covering a hole in the ground next to the owners henhouse.

The hatch for the commanders scissors periscope from a Jagdpanzer IV, one side of the hinge has been welded while the other was bolted to the fighting compartment roof.

The brake access hatch from a Panzer IV, this part still shows quite a large section of the zimmerit coating. There is red primer visible underneath the location of the hinge.

The interior face of the Panzer IV brake acces hatch. Red primer is visible where the hinge was bolted but the main colour of the part is Dunkelgelb.Note: The cooling vent has a wooden plug that was fitted to stop the ingress of mud, water and debris.

This is a very interesting section of Schürzen from a Panzer IV turret, it shows a red outlined Balkenkruez from the 3.PD. There may be part of a red tactical number to the left of the Balkenkreuz, possibly a 3,5,6,8 or nine?

The Flammenvernichter from a Panzer IV J, it was very carefully examined and measured for future reference.

The side access hatches from a Panzer IV, there is one hatch from each side of the turret as indicated by the latch mechanism.

EIN LETZTES VER

Brian Murdoch´s model depicts a somewhat unusual combination of zimmerit coated turret and non-coated hull, painted in the characteristic Daimler-Benz dot pattern camouflage.

Panther 202 - 2/SS.Pz Rgt.1, Stoumont, December 19, 1944

SCHNAUFEN

The German Ardennes offensive of December 1944 has always been the period of WW2 that I have found the most interesting; the units involved, the later production vehicles, the combat and the pivotal nature of the conflict have always attracted me to this point of the war, so my vehicle was always going to be an Ardennes Panther. One particular photo attracted me and that was of Panther 202 abandoned in La Gleize Belgium and after visiting the photo site in 2009 I decided this vehicle would be my model subject.

Historical background

In late 1944 Adolf Hitler decided to launch a counter-offensive against the Allies in the West, this was to take place through the Ardennes region of Eastern Belgium (a route which had been used successfully in 1940). The aim of was to drive a wedge between the US 9th and British 21st armies and the rest of the allies and also in capturing the port of Antwerp .This it was hoped this would result in a mass surrender of allied troops and allow the Germans to regain the initiative in the West. A huge force was secretly built up in anticipation of the attack and on December the 16th 1944 the offensive finally began. One of the primary units involved in this attack was the 1st SS Panzerkorps which had specially reorganised its sub units to spearhead the push forward. Kampfgruppe Peiper would spearhead the advance and had been allocated the tanks of SS Pz.Rgt 1, which included the Panthers of the first and second kompanies. The Panzerkampfwagen Panther Ausf G, Panther 202 belonged to this unit and was commanded by UnterScharfuhrer Hans Friedrich. The Panther of Uscha Friedrich was a Daimler-Benz vehicle built in September 1944 and delivered to the unit as part of the build up to the offensive. It had not seen combat before the Ardennes and had not yet fired a shot in anger. It has some interesting features amongst which are the Daimler-Benz "Dot Pattern" camouflage scheme seen only for a limited time. This was a three colour soft edged sprayed scheme with dots of sand and red brown sprayed over the contrasting colours to break up the pattern and give a light and shadow effect. The turret has been coated on its vertical surfaces with a zimmerit anti magnetic mine coating but the hull has not. I chose to portray an engine deck modification which shows the later central engine deck cover with the holes for the crew compartment heater, although this vehicle does not yet have the high tower fitted. The heater apertures were covered by a rectangular plate, which was bolted in place. This feature is present on Panther 232 of the same unit, which has the same zimmerit turret/bare hull combination and is from the same production period. It is possible that the engine decks arrived at the assembly plant before the tower castings, we shall probably never know. The Panther also shows the distinctive spare track hangers fitted on Panthers from SS Pz.Rgt 1. made from round bar "U" shapes welded onto the turret by the maintenance unit. The turret numbers in black with a broken white outline are also typical of SS-Pz Rgt.1 and the smaller

The subject of the article. Archive photos of 202 after it was abandoned out of fuel in La Gleize ,the colour scheme and zimmerit turret detail are still easily seen. Note the over painting of the spare tracks on the rear hull, and the letter G below them at the lower corner (probably notifying Glysantin or anti freeze has been added to the engine). The distinctive Daimler-Benz "dot" pattern is obvious in both photos

CEGESOMA

LA GLEIZE, THE ARDENNES

This then and now photo was taken in 2009. The building has been whitewashed but the distinctive brick patterns under the roof edge and the coping where the white-wash ends are still obvious. The ruined building further up the street has now been replaced.

numbers repeated on the turret upper left rear typical of 2 kompanie vehicles.

Over the next few days the KampfGruppe moved, West regularly changing route and direction as it came across resistance or bridges were blown blocking their progress. They through what are now well known towns and villages such as Honsfeld, Bullingen and Infamous Baugnez crossroads (scene of the Malmedy massacre of US Artillery troops). Their route passed through Stavelot and Trois-Ponts on to La Gleize before finally preparing to attack to the village of Stoumont on the morning of December 19th. At approximately 7am, the Panthers rolled forward taking casualties almost immediately from US 76mm anti tank and 90mm anti aircraft guns.

The attack was pressed on encouraged by the commanders and, with some of the Panthers flanking to the North of the village, resistance was overcome and the majority of Stoumont was secure by 10am. Captured prisoners were returned to the rear and the Kampfgruppe halted briefly, crews and grenadiers taking the opportunity to forage through the houses and vehicles for fuel, food and supplies.

My diorama is set at this point in the story, 202 has stopped in Stoumont, the crew tired but still optimistic at their progress, only the driver looks pensive, a final break to top up a few jerrycans of captured gasoline. Time for a quick smoke of captured American cigarettes, one of Hstf Diefenthal's grenadiers is trying to get some news from an HQ motorcyclist as they try to make sense of the chaos of the battle. In 30 minutes, the Panther would once again on the move, out of Stoumont and West down through the village of Targnon, meeting little resistance and finally to Stoumont station where the Kampfgruppe ran into a strong American position with anti aircraft guns, Sherman tanks and M36 tank destroyers.

The lead Panther was damaged and the crew bailed out, The Germans withdrew until the afternoon when they attacked again losing another 2 Panthers in the process. A stalemate then ensued with the Americans unable to progress because of knocked out vehicles blocking the road and 202 and several other Panthers still active around the Station. Fire was exchanged for most of the day until at 16.00, after darkness had started to fall and an abortive counterattack by the Americans, the surviving Panthers, including 202 withdrew back towards Stoumont where they secured the Western end of the town. They would later withdraw further to La Gleize where 202 was finally abandoned out of fuel on 23rd December, the crew escaping from La Gleize on foot with less than 1000 men of the KG to link up with the German Forces East of Wanne shortly before dawn.

Modelling Panther 202

Before starting, I collected as much reference on Daimler-Benz Panthers as I could including photos of KG Peiper vehicles other "Dot pattern" DB vehicles along with photos of the existing Panther at Grandmenil in Belgium. Although this was not a KG Peiper vehicle, it is a Daimler-Benz Panther with

UPDATES OF THE KIT

1. Cromwell models cupola.
2. Aber set 35K04. Fenders, brackets, barrel etc.
3. Zimmerit from automotive body putty.
4. Accurate Armour Panther detail set A116. (cream coloured resin parts)
5. WWII Productions tracks
6. Suspension adjusted to give the model a better "sit".

DML KIT 6370

many of the same features I would require. Roddy MacDougall also helped greatly in clarifying details and providing advice on the vehicle and camouflage. The base model was Dragon's Steel wheeler kit, which has all the characteristics needed to build this version and includes a set of rubber rimmed tyres. The kit is very good but could still be enhanced with some additional work and aftermarket products. The cast exhaust gaurds have a very pronounced angle at the bottom and need to be sanded to a more rounded profile, likewise the exhaust retaining mounts were changed from the kit type to the type seen on Panther 202 using PE parts from various sets.

The rear idler wheel arms were thinned down and the grease nipple added, the suspension was lowered slightly towards the rear to give the characteristic Panther "sit". All the mudguards were replaced with PE parts which are better for simulating damage, new rivets were added to align correctly with the Accurate Armour schurtzen rail mounts (the same AA set also supplied new thinner hatches, gun travel lock, periscope guards, fire extinguisher, jack block, track re-mounting cable and tow cable mount U brackets for the rear deck). All the tool mounts were re-made from PE (Aber for the most part) with mounting welds added from styrene rod; the gun cleaning tube is also a reworked Aber item with reworked end caps. The spare track rail at the rear was made from styrene strip with Accurate Armour U brackets and styrene rod welds, PE chains and WW2 productions resin track finished this part off.

The zimmerit was made with a technique shown to me by Roddy MacDougall using automotive repair putty and a blade. The turret spare track hangers that come with the kit are incorrect and do not let the spare track hang at the correct height or angle , these were replaced with wire and styrene weld beads and a lot of test fitting to get the correct sit. Aber grills were added to the fans and intakes as well as a retaining strip of styrene around the circular fans. The blocked off heater holes were made with styrene card and some bolt heads. A Cromwell models cupola was used with an Aber barrel and the mantlet was textured to give a more convincing effect, a reworked Dragon anti aircraft mount was also used. Stowage came from the spares box covered with a tarp made from magic sculpt and the vehicle was ready for paint.

After priming with Tamiya fine surface primer the model was painted with Tamiya acrylics the base Dunkelgelb made from a mix of Tamiya Buff, White and Yellow , masks were made from gloss photo paper and held in place with thin blu-tack to allow the spraying of the colour fields which are tight but not quite hard edge. The green was mixed from Tamiya Cockpit Green, Park Green and Deep Green; the red brown was also a Tamiya colour.

The model was then coated in a coat of Johnson's Klear floor polish; this gives a good base for washes and for applying decals which were applied when it was dry. Various oil washes and filters were applied, also weathering with humbrols

to give subtle streaking etc, these vehicles were not very old and had not seen much action so chipping and rusting were kept to a minimum and also achieved with Humbrol enamels and artists oils. Almost all the detail painting was done with Vallejo acrylics; tools, stowage etc were all then given washes and some subtle drybrushing to give some depth. Finally, some pigments were used to tie it all together.

The DKW

The DKW is the Tamiya kit re-worked to depict a late model, photos show the DKW's attached to KG Peiper had no rear seat hence this was removed and some stowage was added in its place. Some photo etch from Voyager enhanced the detail and then it was painted in much the same way as the Panther.

Figures

The figures are all modified in some way with the exception of the grenadier which is a stock Alpine figure painted straight from the box. The Driver is a Dragon figure modified with an Alpine head and Magic-Sculpt scarf, the cupola figure is a re-worked Pegaso item with an Alpine head and the engine deck figure is a hybrid of two Alpine figures using the Peiper figure body and the arms from another Alpine figure in U boat leathers. The Motorcyclist is a scratch built figure made for me by Roddy MacDougall also using a modified Alpine head, all figures were painted in Vallejo acrylics.

Building and base

The building is a generic Ardennes type house based on photos from reference books and on photos taken on my trips to La Gleize and Stoumont.

I first made a framework of plastic card to get the shape and size I wanted. I then cut up stonework from a Miniart building, gradually built up the walls and windows until I was happy with the result. The roof tiles and slates were made individually and laid overlapping each other using the same method as the real ones. The shed doors were made of basswood strip with hinges

Side view on converted Miniart building, pitchfork from Historex, grass from Fredericus Rex, Roof tiles made by hand from plasticard, the building was painted in Vallejo acrylics and weathered with oils.

This photos shows the zimmerit detail, made from Automotive body putty and textured with a converted knife blade, Decals from Archer and tracks from WW2 productions.

202

202

made from plastic card. Detailing and guttering were also scratch built plastic card items and the roof capping was made of lead foil and plastic strip. The woodshed at the end of the house was made from basswood strip and corrugated plastic with some resin logs and a chopping block from Aires. The building was painted and airbrushed entirely in acrylics with oil washes and drybrushing to add depth and highlights. The groundwork was made using exterior filler, sand and white glue mixed together with acrylic paint. The figures and vehicles were pressed into the groundwork before drying and it was then painted with acrylics and semi gloss varnish. Leaves and foliage were added using Hudson and Allen and Fredericus Rex Items.

Acknowledgements

I need to thank Roddy MacDougall for help with Information, photos, zimmerit assistance and especially for the sculpting of the Motorcyclist figure. all the guys in this book really pulled together with advice and ideas but special thanks must also go to Phil and Mirko for their advice and encouragement when the project seemed to be unending. I must also thank Alan Jamieson for letting me raid his bottomless model collection and to Kristof Pulinckx and Herman Vuerstaek for being dragged around the Ardennes and answering questions on all things Belgian during my information quest. Finally I must thank Markus Lack for advice on translations and the diorama title.

Brian Murdoch

EIN LETZTES VERSCHNAUFEN

202

INFRA RED PREPARED PANTHER (B

VISIBLE EXTERNAL FEATURES AND CHARACTERISTICS

Gunnar Jansson used his professional engineering skills to create his own photo etch that he used to update his interpretation of an IR prepared Panther. He also explains the method used to obtain the dimensions for the rather mysterious IR box revealing some new information that is being published for the first time.

WA)

BIWA Panther from I.Pz.Rgt 6 (3.PD) knocked out by two 85 mm projectiles, at the cemetery in Hercegfalva (known today as Mezöfalva) during the Konrad III operation. The 3.PD suffered high losses here, including more than 6 Panthers during an intense counterattack. Photo taken in February 1945.

BIWA Panther from I.Pz.Rg. 6 "Kgr. Weymann", probably destroyed in the area north of Stuhlweissenburg (Szekesfehervar) in Hungary 1945 during Konrad III.

A Panther assembled by Daimler-Benz who positioned the Balkenkreuz between the hammer and track maintenance tools on the starboard side. This Panther was knocked out during the Konrad III operation and most probably belonged to I/Pz.Rgt 6.

A later DB BIWA Panther from I.Pz.Rgt. 24, knocked out in the Pettend area at the end of January 1945. Note the spare wheel brackets fitted to the turret rear and the late flammenvernichter exhausts.

IR (Infra Red) or BIWA (Bild Wandler) which is the German term used for equipment that enables the user to see objects that generate a different heat signature to its surroundings, thereby giving the user the ability to operate in darkness. The Panther was one of the vehicles that it was planned would be equipped with these devices and from September 1944 some of the Panthers produced were adapted to use this IR equipment.

I have had plans to build an IR or IR-prepared Panther for quite some time now. As information, data and photos had been very scarce, this project was shelved until enough information became available. This situation had not changed much until I was asked to contribute an article for this "Panther Special" book. I felt the time was right for me to have a go at tackling this subject and that my contribution for the book would be a "BIWA" Panther.

I started my research by going through the material I had amassed, mainly photos but also some intelligence reports describing how the IR equipment functioned. There is also anecdotal evidence that suggests for example, that the IR sights did not function properly in rain and snow. More information has surfaced and with the help and assistance of friends, I have had the opportunity to analyse some new and unpublished photos, which has really helped this project. With the help of the new photos and discussions with Hilary Doyle and Roddy MacDougall I was able reach some conclusions. Some of these are my own interpretation of what can be seen and should not be taken as the final "word" on the subject.

There are four main external features that can be observed in photos of BIWA Panthers, these are well known to anyone with an interest in the subject.

External features seen on IR (BIWA) Panthers:

BIWA Panthers in the Village of Kocs west of Tatabánya in late December 1944. They are either from I.Pz.Rgt 6 or I.Pz.Lehr.Rgt 130. Note the style of the turret numbers and the September Daimler Benz "licht und schatten" spot overlay to the camouflage scheme.

INFRA RED PREPAR

- An armoured stowage box on the starboard side of the rear armour plate, replacing the standard stowage bin.
- Two rectangular mounting tabs on the starboard side of the gun mantlet.
- A horseshoe shaped armoured guard on the turret roof in front of cupola that provides protection for elevation band aperture.
- There is no cupola hatch handle to allow a 360 degree rotation of IR sight by the commander. This was either removed during the vehicles IR preparation, or perhaps not fitted at the assembly plant.

I have come to the conclusion that when a post September production Panther has no handle fitted to the commanders hatch, there is a strong possibility that this is an IR prepared Panther that will have all these other features as well.

Armoured IR box

The armoured storage box is a bit of a mystery when it comes to its internal features and how the equipment was actually stowed inside. Photos that have surfaced of this box show only a fraction of the interior with a couple of mounting straps or brackets. As new photos keeps appearing especially those from former eastern block archives, hopefully one day we will find out more about the interior fittings of this box. We know the external features of the box more or less, but still we lack clear photos of the locking mechanism and the strange "brackets" seen on top of the box in some photos. These brackets were probably used for stowage of some kind, but we can only speculate as to what they may have stored. I will now stick my neck out and say that we have gathered enough information and data to establish the external dimensions and features of the box. I would say the IR box was not any bigger than the standard stowage bin. It could have been slightly

2 x Photo Archives of Museum of Military History in Budapest / Elek Wojnarovich

deeper but only by a couple of centimetres. Looking at photos, the box may look deeper than it actually is, but I think this is an optical illusion caused by the fact that the box is not as tall as the standard stowage bin. I will explain how I came to this conclusion; the box itself has very similar dimensions to those of the standard stowage bin apart from its height. There is a step in the standard bin where the locking clasps are located, if the dimensions of the standard bin up to this "step" are transferred to the IR box they are more or less identical, but we will come back to this later. The IR box was assembled from 14mm armoured steel plate that was welded together, it had a hinged hatch that was locked with a threaded bolt and locking handle. The exact design of the locking mechanism has not yet been verified, my drawing is an educated guess based on what can be seen in the available photos. There was a small rectangular plate welded to the front face on the leading edge of the door on the IR box, this had a slot cut into it that accepted the threaded bolt and locking handle. There was another small plate with a hole that made up part a hasp for a padlock welded underneath the locking handle plate but on the edge of the door. There was a corresponding plate welded to the side of the box. The padlock would have provided extra security for the IR equipment that was still classified as secret. The box was bolted to four square mounting studs welded to the hull rear plate.

IR prepared Panthers were assembled by all three manufacturing plants involved in the Panther program, M.A.N., Daimler-Benz and M.N.H. From examining photos of IR Panthers from these assembly plants, we can see that there are two mounting positions for the IR box on the Panthers rear plate. Some Panther have the bottom of the IR box level with the sponson plate and others have it level with the engine deck. The common denominator with these latter Panthers is that they all show vehicles built by M.A.N. One picture can be seen on page 190 of the Schiffer book on the 1st Pz. Div. It can

Close up of the rear of Panther on page 107. Note the jerry can holder between the stowage bin and exhaust. Unfortunately, we can only see a fraction of the box's internal features.

Mirko Bayerl Collection

Part of the 3-D CAD model incorporated in one of the photos to match the proportions of the CAD model to the photo.

The 3-D CAD version of the IR box.

My scratched build master before going into the silicone mould. The weld seams were made with "brown stuff" epoxy putty from Kneadatite.

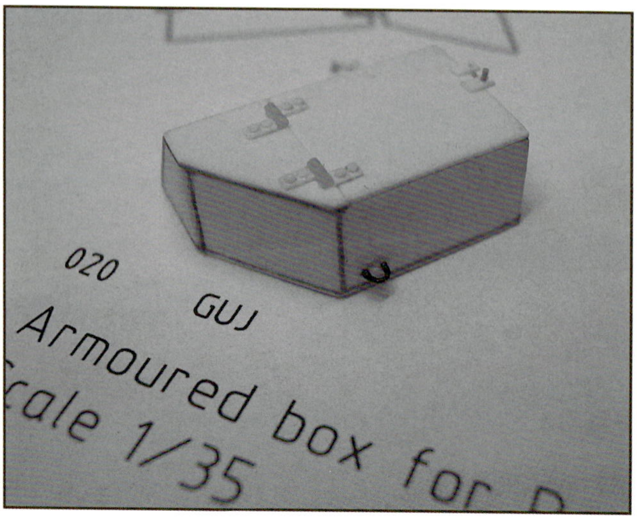

also seen in an unpublished Befehlspanther photograph from a private collection. The Befehlspanther photographed in Krefelt on page 5-193 of panzertracts No 5-3 has the mounting studs for the IR box welded in a position that would have the IR box sitting level with the engine deck. No Panthers from Daimler-Benz or M.N.H. have been seen with the IR box mounted in the higher position, when the IR box is fitted to Panthers assembled by either of these firms they are invariably mounted level with the sponson.

It is also common to see a lifting eye welded to the top of the IR box. This eye is positioned close to the centre of gravity on the box, near the back and to the right hand side. Having the eye in this position would keep the box level and make it tilt towards the rear plate when lifted to ease mounting it to the rear hull plate.

Determing the IR box dimensions

Working with CAD (Computer Aided Design) in my profession I had an idea on how I it might be possible to check the exterior dimensions of the IR box. I started with a parametric 3-D model of the box, this allows you to automatically change size and features by changing dimensional values. The method I used for determining the external dimensions is not exact by any means but this is how I did. I took some of the photos I had and used them as a background in the CAD. I then implemented the CAD model in "space" over the boxes in the photos, trying to align the edges of the model with the ones in the background photo. I tried different sizes of the box, adjusting both width and depth to those of the standard stowage box but none of them would match the pictures properly. Keeping the width, depth the same as the standard stowage bin and height as described earlier made the best match that was almost spot on.

Kampfgruppe Weymann

The idea to build a Panther from Kampfgruppe Weymann came about

Some of the etched and machined parts I designed and had made. The etched parts were made in the appropriate brass thickness in order get the correct scale thickness for the part.

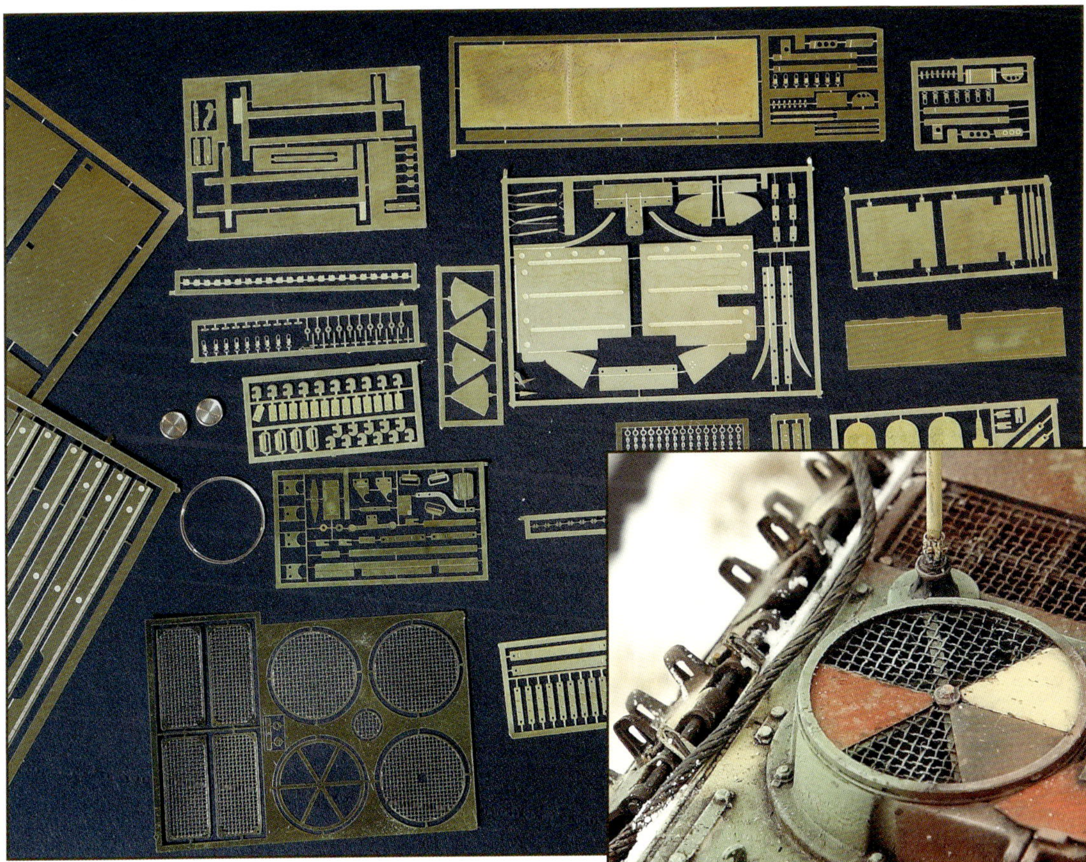

Close up of the crew heater. The mesh screens and panels are author's own design of photo etch. The upper ring is machined in brass and has the correct profile; it even has the small slots cut in to the periphery for locating the panels. The empty shell casing is from RB models, it was blackened and then the patina was revealed using fine steel wool.

during a field trip to Hungary in 2008. I spent a day in the area of Zamoly, north of Szekesfehervar, Szekesfehervar was known as Stuhlweissenburg at the time.

At the beginning of January 1945 Zamoly was the scene of intense fighting. The I.Kav.Korps and III Panzer Korps had been tasked with creating a diversionary attack between the Vertes Mountains and Stuhlweissenburg. This was part of a plan to draw Russian Forces away from the IV-SS.Panzer Korps sector during operation Konrad, the attempt to relieve the encircled city of Budapest. The two Korps had under their command the following Divisional and additional units, 1 Pz.Div, 3 Pz.Div, 23 Pz.Div, 4 Kav.Brig and S.Pz.Abt 503 (Tiger). The Korps also had Assault Guns and Werfer units.

Kampfgruppe Weymann had been formed as a rapid strike force from the various Divisional units of the 3 Pz.Div. The Kampfgruppe consisted of I/Pz.Rgt 6 under the command of either Hauptmann Fiehl or Hauptmann Schramm, Pz.Gren. Rgt 3 and elements of Pz.Art.Rgt 75. The Kampfgruppe was under the command of Oberstleutnant Weymann and would see heavy fighting around Gyulamajor, Borbalamajor and Borbala Psz.

The Russians moved the I. Guards Mechanized Corps into the Zamoly area in order to mount a counter attack. Oberstleutnant Weymann had prepared an ambush for the Russians, his troops were placed in well concealed positions giving them an excellent field of fire. The Russians walked straight into the trap. During this battle the Germans claimed to have knocked out 50 Russian lend lease Sherman tanks. Some reports estimate the number to be somewhat higher at between 60 to 80 tanks. During the intense fire from the Germans, the Russian Sherman's crews panicked and could not turn or withdraw due to the ice and snow on the incline. They were an easy target for the experienced German tank commanders.

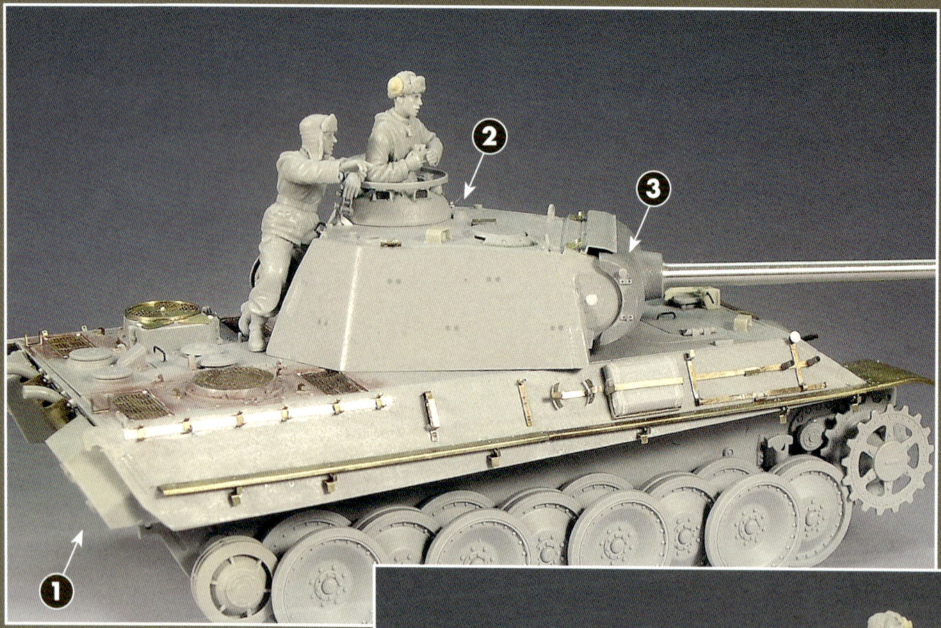

EXTERNAL FEATURES OF AN IR-PREPARED PANTHER

1. The armoured stowage box on starboard rear armour plate which replaced the standard stowage bin.
2. Horse shoe shaped armoured guard on turret roof in front of cupola that provided protection for the handle of the IR elevation band on the turret.
3. The two rectangular mounting brackets on the right side of the gun mantlet associated with IR prepared Panthers.
4. The absence of a handle on the cupola hatch allows the IR equipment to rotate through 360 degrees independently of the turrets traverse.

On the right page we see the same features on the finished model.

Here we can see a mix of updates from Armorscale, resin parts from Accurate Armour, and the author's design of etched and machined parts along with other scratch built parts.

The crew figures were sculpted on to "mannequins" made from an etched armature with resin parts for the torso and pelvis. The masters for the figures were sculpted with Magic Sculpt and the heads are reworked Hornet heads. The figures in the photos are resin copies of the originals.

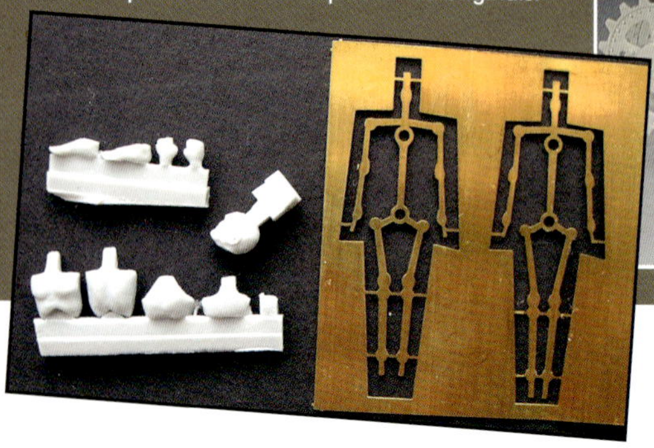

A Swedish Volunteer, Nils Rosén who served in 7 Kompanie, II. /Pz.Rgt 6, was a Panzer IV commander and remembered the battle in his personal diary as follows ' an impressive and pretty sight seeing all the slowly burning wrecks lighting up the landscape at night'. During the field trip in 2008, we actually managed to conduct some excavations in the area, we found a Pz IV shell casing, MG ammunition and several egg hand grenades, but most important of all we were able to find the ambush positions of Kampfgruppe Weymann and observe the open terrain where the Russians had lost so many Sherman tanks.

Oberstleutnant Martin Weymann was awarded the Knights Cross in February 1945 for this action, however during March 1945 he was badly wounded during an engagement in the Seregelyes/Mihaly Major area. He later died from his wounds in a Military Hospital in Austria. The Commander of the 2./Pz.Rgt 6 Leutnant Albert Blaich was also killed when his Panther was hit several times after being ambushed by an SU 100.

The Panthers of I/Pz.Rgt 6 had arrived in Hungary during December 1944 to re join their parent unit the 3. Pz.Div. One other Panther Abteilung also returned to its parent division in Hungary, I/Pz.Rgt 11 which returned to the 6.Pz Div. A further Panther Abteilung arrived in Hungary in December I/Pz.Lehr.Rgt 130. In January 1945 the personnel I/Pz.Lehr.Rgt 130 was ordered back to Germany to form part of a reformed Panzer Lehr Regiment and handed over its tanks to I/Pz.Rgt 1 and II/Pz.Rgt 23.

These units were supposed to have been equipped with infrared devices, but actually, there are no confirmed reports of IR Panthers being used in Hungary. In fact, prior to their transportation to Hungary these units were ordered to remove all of their IR equipment. There were many reasons for this but one of them was that the equipment was still technically unreliable and did not work in a snowy conditions. However, there

is an unconfirmed report that Versuchszug Haas under command of leutnant Haas, attached to the 1 Kompanie, Pz.Lehr. Rgt 130 did use four IR equipped Panthers, but this has not been confirmed. Another IR prepared Panther Abteilung in Hungary was I/Pz.Rgt 24. This unit arrived in Hungary during mid January 1945 just in time for the start of the Konrad III operation and was attached to Pz.Rgt 1 of the 1 Pz.Div most of the time. There are no report of this unit using IR in field.

However in March 45, the 3./Pz.Rgt 6 returned to Hungary after a short refit, they had complete sets of IR equipment installed and were ready for action. They were however ordered to remove all of their IR equipment and load it on a train for transport back to Germany. The reason was the rapidy advancing Russian Army and the fear it would fall in to their hands.

There are some photographs of Panthers taken in the small of Village of Kocs, just West of Tatabanya (Panthers 321, 221 and the wreck of 133). These pictures were taken during December 1944 and show IR mounts on the tanks. After extensive research it has been determined that these Panthers came from either I/Pz.Rgt 6 or Pz.Lehr.Rgt 130. I personally believe them to be from I/Pz.Rgt 6.

The Panther I decided to build was a typical Daimler-Benz production vehicle made during October or November 1944. The Panther came with a factory applied camouflage scheme and some additional features; I wanted to add a red and black Balkenkreuz. This type of Balkenkreuz was seen with armoured vehicles serving on the Eastern Front in 44/45. The reason for a red and black painted Balkenkreuz is still not clear, but I assume it may have been to make it less of an aiming point when compared to the standard white and black Balkenkreuz.

Scenario

It is the second week of January 1945 on the outskirts of Zamoly, the day is foggy and the ground is frozen. The mud is hard with a layer of snow; it had been snowing for the last 2 days. A Biwa Panther from 2 Kompanie, Pz.Rgt 6 lays in ambush (2 Kp was commanded by Knights Cross holder Leutnant Albert Blaich). The Panther commander is surveying the area in anticipation of a strong Russian attack or the singal for them to start their own attack. This is the calm before the storm.

Building the Panther

The Panther I have built represents a Daimler Benz vehicle produced in late October or early November 44, with a factory applied camouflage pattern. Daimler-Benz adopted this pattern in September 1944; Daimler-Benz then used this basic scheme throughout the war. Another feature adopted by the Daimler-Benz factory was the camouflage painted spare track links. The air flow regulation louvers on the starboard air intake grills were not fitted. These louvers started to appear in photos

The snow was made from polyester granulate mixed with white glue and water that was then applied with a brush. Note how the it has settled in corners and crevices.

from 1945 and it seems were on Panthers produced in December 44 at earliest. My representative Panther has been on training grounds and has been involved in combat since arrival in Hungary in December 1944, it is now a few days into 1945 with snow laying on the ground. Even though tanks are beaten up quickly, I wanted to represent a fresh vehicle, as it has only been in combat for a few weeks.

The DML panther kits are the most recent and accurate on the market today. They are very good when it comes to shape and dimensions and the detail is very nice overall. It has some minor issues here and there that could have been made a little better but overall they are very nice kits. The best value for money is in my opinion Dragons Steel wheel Panther kit 6370, as you get both the early and late exhaust stacks, but above all you also get the normal rubber rimmed wheel's, this kit formed the base for my build.

The first I did was apply different textures to the appropriate areas, simulating armoured plate using my normal method of stippling on liquid glue with a cheap soft round brush like the cheap ones kids use for watercolour. I use Humbrol liquid poly but other brands would do, if I want a rougher texture as found on cast items I just use a stiffer brush. I brush the glue on, as it starts to dry pretty quickly I work on small areas at a time like a turret side. I more or less just wet the area and using the soft brush stipple the surface, when the brush starts to stick to the surface or make small lumps I rinse the brush and it's time to add more glue. After the glue has set over night I used a motor tool with a small round ball nose cutter and gently add some more texture in a random pattern bouncing the cutter lightly on the surface. Here it is important not to exaggerate by making large dents and above all do not "slip" with the cutter. This is easily done if you are not careful and the result will be a pitted line that does not look realistic and makes it look exactly like what it is, a manually applied surface treatment.

After that, the assembly was quite straight forward, but here I would like to mention a tip I received from fellow modeller and friend Roddy MacDougall. As the upper hull tends to warp, I glued two styrene beams to the inner face of the hull deck, at the back and front of the turret aperture. This will ensure that the hull deck remains flat when the upper and lower hull are glued together, this will prevent the unnatural gap that may otherwise occur between the hull deck and the turret that can be caused by the deck flexing. I used WW2 production tracks for the main tracks, but Master Club tracks for the spare track links.

Using my own design of Photo etch

I wanted to upgrade my Panther and make it as accurate as possible. There are several companies that manufacture photo etch sets designed to upgrade the Dragon Panther. I was not satisfied with the dimensions and features on many parts in these sets. One

Left view showing the DB camo pattern. The storage tube was photo etched with two weld seams added as the length of the original tube was made from three pieces. The schurtzen was photo etched using 0.15mm brass.

of the things that is not available in any of the commercially available etched sets was the correct thickness of the etched sheet used for parts like tool racks, jack mount, late Flammenvernichter exhaust brackets etc, these didn't have the heavier "bulk" I wanted to depict these parts properly. All of these sets had these parts etched in same thickness of brass as the majority of the other details, a compromise made to keep the cost down. I could not find any appropriately sized gas detector panels for the turret in any of these sets so this was high on my priority list. I later also added the small wingnuts found on the gas detector panels, these are very small and delicate parts but with patience and a good pair of tweezers they can be added to the model. There are a few brands on the market today and they all have advantages and disadvantages. They are generally good, but there is always a compromise when it comes to rendering the parts in their appropriate scale thicknesses. This quite understandable when looking at it from a manufactures perspective, making the parts in their correct scale thicknesses would make the sets more complicated and expensive to produce.

I have a contact who has designed etched parts for model railway kits and display models; I saw an opportunity to design my own parts for the Dragon Panther G kit with his help.

I started with a few parts, but more parts were added as I went along, the range eventually increased to not only encompass etched parts but also machined parts in the end. The good thing of designing your own parts is that now I had the opportunity to have the parts made in the appropriate scale thickness. The initial cost for photo etching can be quite high depending on what contact you have and where they are made. You normally need to make a couple of test runs before getting the parts exactly as you want them, there always seems to be something you have missed or something that would be better if it was done a different way.

As I had started to build my Panther before the parts were ready, some of the parts I have designed have not been used on the model for this book. I did not use the front fenders, side rails and schurzen hangers, here I used Armorscale parts that I had already had fitted and I thought looked okay. Armorscale's side rails are too long as they were designed for the Tamiya kit, I needed to correct the length of the rear section and adapt it to fit the Dragon kit. Another part I decided to keep was the guard over the mantlet, I had thinned out the plastic part from the kit which looked okay. The plate thickness I used for

To get some variations in the crew´s clothing the author used different garment pattern and colours. The tow cables are from Karaya. Note the red and black Balkenkreuz, a feature sometimes seen on the eastern front. The reason for using this colour combination is unknown but an educated guess is that it made them a less obvious aiming point for the Soviet gunners.

my parts was from 0.15-0.3 mm, the engine intake screens would have benefitted from being made in 0.1 mm, I would consider doing this for my next production run. One major improvement I have made is the crew heater detail, especially the ring that I had machined in brass; this has the correct "L" cross section and has the grooves machined at the periphery to locate the pie shaped air regulation panels. Having this ring machined in one piece made the part more accurate and the assembly so much easier compared to the delicate assembly needed for the multiple parts used in commercial photo etch sets.

The IR storage box and upgrading the jack block

From my CAD data, I scratch built a master using plastic card using epoxy putty for the weld seams. The jack block was updated from the Tamiya kit part as I had started one earlier on which I had scribed a wood pattern and added metal bands. I now added the lifting handle which is a feature often missed by modellers and kit manufactures, all jack blocks had a lifting handle.

Moulds were made of the parts and copies cast in resin so that they might be used for future projects.

Painting

I started my paint job by applying a blackish brown pre shading, concentrating on the lower hull parts. After this had dried, I applied the camouflage scheme using Tamiya acrylics, thinned with lacquer thinner which works well with these paints. I used mixes for all three colours keeping the shades on the light side as the weathering process will darken them. I did not want my colours to be too light, I was making a winter scene and wanted a cold and murky look for my vignette.

If the colours were too light I feared they would look strange and not have enough contrast with the snow. For the green, I used Tamiya XF-58 Olive green with XF-15 Flesh but also some white and yellow to lighten it. Using flesh gives the colour a warmer hue that is more to my liking. For the dark yellow I used XF-60 Dark yellow I used some white with a little flesh to get a tone that I liked. For the red brown, XF-64 Red brown was the base with some XF-9 Hull red mixed in and lightened with XF-15 Flesh. Before I painted the model, I had drawn the camouflage pattern on paper as a first step. I also had a old Tamiya Panther build that I used as a test bed for checking the colours, pattern and airbrush settings. A very good tip is to have a spare model as a test bed before going on to the real model. After the basic camo was laid on I sprayed

This was the author's first attempt at painting an entire figure in acrylics in 1/35, he used the Andrea "flesh" and "white" painting sets which worked well. The headphones are from Tasca, the binoculars straps were made using thin metal foil. The turret numbers were masked with a custom made template and then sprayed with acrylics.

The ladder was soldered using 0.5m brass rod and photo etched side profiles, it was then secured to the vehicle with a track pin from Adler's nest. The spare tracks are from Master Club.

the turret numbers using paint stencils kindly made for me by a Hungarian friend Ottó Józsa, I first sprayed a black base, masked the "center" and then sprayed the white outline. The Balkenkreuz were also sprayed using stencils that I had cut myself.

When the base was fully dry, I applied a gloss coat using Johnson's Klear, this makes a good protective base for the weathering process. Having a semi gloss or glossy surface made the next step, the washes easier to apply and more controllable. The wash does not "spread" so much and flows easily, it is also easier to remove if need be.

I used Citadel paint thinned with some water and Klear for some pin washes, the Klear acts as a flow agent and prevents "ring marks" from forming after the wash is dry. I got this tip from a very nice book from "Imperial Armour Model masterclass" volume one from Forge world, written by Phil Stuchinskas and Mark Bedford. This book deals with Warhammer figures and vehicles but the models and their painting and weathering are stunning, a lot of great tips and ideas and highly recommended. After applying some more pin washes including some made using MIG shadow brown oil colour I added a matt clear coat.

I continued the weathering process by adding some scratch marks. Both the "sponge" technique and brush painting were used for this. I used a mix of "chaos black" and "Scorched brown" from the Citadel acrylic range, some marks were also made using enamels too. Highlights were added here and there using some light drybrushing and picking out certain areas with a fine brush.

Mud

Even though my build should represent a new tank, I wanted to replicate a tank that even in its limited combat experience, shows signs of being through mud, rain and now snow and freezing temperatures. I kept most of my mud colours in a lighter "dry" or "semidry" tone because of the low temperatures. For the mud I mixed acrylic resin, water, plaster, fine sand and pastels. I added the mixture on the wheels, behind the wheels and on the lower and side of the hull with a brush.

I discovered that I had added too much plaster as when the mixture dried, it was too light in colour so that I had to repaint the muddy areas. I did this with Humbrol 187 "dark stone" and the MIG oil colours, dark mud and shadow brown to simulate areas with more moisture.

Snow

As the scene is a winter setting I needed to add snow, not only to the ground itself

The mud was created my applying a mix of acrylic resin, plaster, pastels and fine sand. When dry it was painted with Humbrol 187 Dark stone and oils to achieve the desired colour variations.

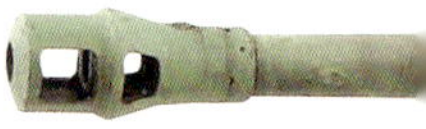

Another view of the IR box from a different angle. Note the handle and the locking mechanism. Home made photo etched exhaust covers were used as the aftermarket ones at the time protruded too far out from the casted protectors, they should be almost flush with these.

but I also wanted to add some snow lying on appropriate areas of the vehicle where it has "collected" after snowfalls. Here one has to think logically about where to apply the snow, how it collects at certain spots, how the wind and weather conditions have melted and moved it around. It is important not to overdo it, add a little and build it up gradually. I made good use of the book "Endkampf um das Reichgebiet" from "Start-Luftvart verlag as reference, it has some pictures showing panthers with the sow effect I was after. To make the small snow patches I used polyester granulate, a material kindly given to me by Brian Murdoch, who had in turn received it from the Dutch modeller Hugo Luyten. Hugo had used it on a stunning Humvee diorama in an Afghanistan setting in 2006. It is a very fine granule product, much finer than micro balloons and is almost like icing sugar. This was mixed with some white glue and water and applied on the model using a fine brush.

Figures

I had different thoughts regarding the scene and number of figures figure's I would need. The time limit for this book project made me decide on a "simple" approach, with a simplified base and only a couple of figures. The figures I used were free sculpted except for the heads which are re worked Hornet heads. I normally sculpt my own figures completely from scratch, after I came up with an idea for the poses I started to sculpt on a 1/35th scale armature I had etched along with some resin parts used for the torso and pelvis. I copied the idea from Andrea who have a similar armature for their 54mm (1/32nd scale) figure range. I sculpted a pelvis, torso, feet, hand palms and a basic head from magic sculpt, these original parts was then casted for use in future projects. I had decided the look of the figures early on, inspired by a couple of photos of the Swedish volunteer Nils Rosén and other crew members from Pz. Reg 6. They were all wearing the characteristic fur caps and padded winter clothing. The head on the pointing figure was later replaced by a re worked Hornet head as I wasn't satisfied with the face of the initial sculpt I had made. I added a sculpted fur cap to this Hornet head which I found suitable. The commanders head is also a slightly re worked Hornet head. It could have been used as stock item as it already had a basic "fur cap", but I wanted more volume for the fur so I added more using magic sculpt. All the sculpting was done using Magic sculpt and Kneadatite or a mix of both on some details. I use simple tools for my sculpting,

like shaped wooden toothpicks and a calliper needle in a drawing pen occasionally.

My favourite knife blade is a Swann Morton surgical blade number 15C, this is a small curved blade that flexes and bends and follows the curvature in the folds in clothing for example when one wants to sharpen up certain details and areas. When the figures were finished, they were adapted for moulding and casting, the arms were separated. Resin castings were made of the figures as I did not want to paint the "masters" and I had a future use for the figures as base for conversions etc.

Painting

I started by giving the figures a primer coat with Citadel skull white. Next the faces was painted using the Andrea acrylic "Flesh paint set", I wanted to try this set and as a novice at painting with acrylics I thought it would make it a bit easier for me to have good mixes from the beginning. The uniforms were also painted with acrylics, for the white jacket I used the Andrea "white painting set". The rain marks on the splinter pattern were painted with a

An overview of the engine deck. Note the red primer base under the turret, exposed on the starboard side where the turret is traversed. One should consider the turret position when the camouflage was applied, when the turret is moved the underlying colour would be exposed on some vehicles. The gas detection panels are the author's own design, as he couldn't find any on the market with the correct dimensions that matched the information in Panzertracts. Note also the jack block lifting handle.

mix of oil and Humbrol enamels, this has a slower drying time and made them easier to remove if needed.

Groundwork

I wanted to make a small base showing snow on the ground, as I had added some snow on the vehicle I needed to harmonize this to the base, otherwise the snow would look strange or illogical. With a snow covered base it would look more natural... or that was my plan.

As time was running out for the project and I kept the base quite simple, I wanted a snow covered ground with some grass showing through. The groundwork was built up with sculptamold, a papier-mâché type material that you mix with some water, if worked out very nicely. After it had dried I airbrushed it with different earth tone colours mixed from Tamiya acrylics, after which a wash with the MIG oil colours "dark shadow" and some "dark mud" were applied. When dry I brushed on some thinned white glue, sprinkled static grass and added some grass tufts from Joefix-studio. Some small roots were then added. When this was dry I sprinkled on Joefix -studio snow, which looked very convincing as a light snow cover. I wanted to use this product to make a heavier snow layer and tried to mix it with white glue and water, here I discovered it wouldn't mix properly so I ended up using the polyester granulate I had used earlier which worked better. I applied this in a couple of thin layers to get the desired effect I was after.

Thanks

I would like to thank Mirko Bayerl for providing the technical information regarding the function of the IR equipment, historical information and picture content of my article. Special thanks should also go to Otto′ Jozsa, a great Hungarian model builder for designing and making the turret number masks. I would also like to thank Hilary Doyle for his help and Roddy MacDougall for providing detailed information on the Panther some of which is being published for the first time as well as providing hints and tips during my build.

Gunnar Jansson

A view of the front of the Panther. Note the thinned down driver's hatch that is 0.5mm thick compared to the original kit part's 1.7mm.

A photo of a Wiking Panther in Poland featuring some unusual field modifications provided inspiration for Markus Eriksson. The result is a carefully executed copy of the original vehicle.

Modellers seem to be more fascinated with German tanks more than those that were produced by any other nation. The heavier vehicles like the Panther and Tiger are of particular interest. One of the reasons for this might be the total hopelessness and desperation that faced the German forces in the last years of the Second World War. The battles on the Eastern Front fought in 1943 – 1945, when the Germans were forced to retreat by the increasing might of the Soviet army, led to the German government to promises of more and more 'wonder weapons', to help save the German people and reestablish balance of power in Europe. We know all too well the result of this policy, but still we are fascinated by the ingenuity of German engineers during this era. The continued development of the Tiger and Panther in the face of adversity is one of the reasons that these vehicles have held such interest for modellers for so long.

I personally have no single area of expertise relating to a particular unit or period during the war; I try to find a suitable project and then read all that I can find about the subject. This was also the case when I decided to build a Panther. It all started from an idea to build a tank used by the SS

TO HELL AND BACK

Panther Ausf. A, 5. SS. Pz.Div.Wiking, Poland 1944

Division Wiking. One of the distinguishing aspects of this unit is that they operated solely and continuously on the Easter Front, compared to other divisions who were used as 'fire brigades', being thrown into battle wherever they were needed the most. Many of the men belonging to the Wiking division were volunteers from other countries who believed that the Soviet communism was a threat to European existence.

Modellers today have a tendency to show more battle damage, wear and weathering on their models than is evident in photographs of the 'real thing'. Chipped and faded paint in particular are overemphasized. I have read or heard somewhere that a tank's life span after its deployment was around three months. As an example I would like to quote Tomas L. Jentz in his book "Panther Tank: The quest for combat supremacy", 1995:"... *a total of 841 Panthers arrived on the Eastern front in 1943 for employment with the Panther-abteilungen. As of 31 December 1943, 217 of these Panthers had survived of which 80 were operational. A total of 624 (74 percent) were lost as total write offs in 1943."*

It is of course very difficult to determine the exact time span for the survival of a particular tank. Examples exist of vehicles that were put into service early in the war and survived through to 1945. However the quotation from Mr. Jentz shows the level of Panther losses for the German units on the Eastern Front during the middle of the war. We also need to bear in mind that not all of the vehicles rolling of the assembly lines were shipped directly to the front. New vehicles were also issued to training schools, new units that were being raised as well as units that were withdrawn for rest and re equipment. German industry was also suffering badly from the effect of allied bombing and the lack of raw materials. During this period of the war, units were not engaged in battle continuously. This was often the case in the latter stages of the war, particularly on the Eastern front where the Germans were so hard pressed that every working vehicle was needed as soon as it arrived

The story behind the build

When I take on a new project, I usually begin by collecting as many references I can find. My idea for this project was to build a specific tank, which inspired me to make it as realistic as possible.

One of the reasons for selecting this particular Panther A was that I had purchased the book "SS Armour on the eastern front 1943-1945" which has numerous photographs taken on the Eastern front. Among these I found three inspiring images of Panther number 521 from the "Wiking" division taken in Poland during the summer battles of 1944. The fact that the images were not taken on the same occasion, but showed

This photo of Panther 521 was taken outside Warsaw in October 1944 after the fierce summer battles. The side skirts have probably been replaced as they show no signs of wear or battle damage. Note the U brackets and the modified front fenders.

the tank both in the initial stages of the battle and later as the fighting had decreased in the autumn of 1944 heightened my interest in this particular Panther.

One of the interesting things about this vehicle is that it was still operational after the summer and autumn battles; this fact was obvious from the pictures. I studied the pictures to see if there were any unique details for this vehicle or unit and I was thrilled to find several that made it extraordinary from a modelling perspective. The first thing I noticed was the diagonally cut fenders which gives the Panther a stream lined look. The reason for this is unclear, but perhaps it was easier for the crew to climb on to the tank when the schurtzen were fitted. Panther 521 is one of several tanks from the Wiking division with this modification. Another specific detail on this vehicle is the "U" shaped brackets welded to the rear of the engine deck. I had noticed these brackets on Panther 522 from the same unit, I believe these acted as a support for the wooden beams used to put under the tracks when the tank was stuck..

By studying the images and other sources regarding German tank production and development, I worked out that this Panther was probably assembled around November or December 1943. Details that indicate this are the radio operator's Kugelblende, the lack of turret pistol ports and the presence of the twin air cooling pipes on either side of the left hand exhaust. Other details associated with later production models of the Ausf 'A' were missing which were also factored in to my calculation. According to the sources I have at hand, The Wiking division should have received Panther '521' in late December 1943 or early January 1944. Its crew would then have trained on it until they finally went into action a couple of months later.

Panther 521 had its combat debut on the Eastern Front in March or April 1944 during the fighting around Kovel where the Wiking division fought together with the 4th Panzer Division. The tank was a part of the fifth company led by Commander Karl Heinz Lichte. Lichte later became

Collection Andreas Szeibert

We are not certain why the fenders were cut at an angle, a possible explanation can be seen in this photo. It was easier for the crew to climb up on the Panther with the extra "footstep" that the missing section of fender has created. This is Panther 501 in Poland, late 1944.

Max K. via Mirko Bayerl

During the breakout from the Jenö pocket in Hungary on the night of the 22/23 March 1945, the Wiking Division lost several Panthers. Here we can see a knocked out Panther from either 5 Komp. or 6.Komp with modified fenders.

A close up showing the modified fender of a Wiking Panther destroyed in Hungary in 1945.

Another Panther from Wiking abandoned and blown up by its crew along the corridor of death, the breakout from the Jenö pocket. Here we can clearly see the modified fende. This Panther is from the 5. or 6. Kompany, II. SS.Pz.Rgt 5 was formed 1945 with two Kompanies instead of four. The place today has not changed much. Several pieces from the Panther were found here during a field trip.

Max K. via Mirko Bayerl

an Abteilung commander in the Panzer Regiment. The fifth company was the last Wiking unit to appear outside Kovel,where the battle had been raging since the beginning of April. I have no information on who might have been 521's commander during its time of service.

The first images of Panther 521, are from Poland before the big Soviet summer offensive of July 1944. When operation Bagation was launched on June 22, it annihilated 28 German Divisions from Army Group Mitte. To fill the gaps in the front Field Marshall Model summoned the 4th, 5th and 7th Panzer Divisions, the Hermann Göring Fallschirm Panzer Division, the Totenkopf Division and the Wiking Division. It took a considerable period of time to move all of these divisions in order to repulse the Soviet forces. This resulted in battle weary troops being forced to fight more or less constantly all summer.

SS Panzer Regiment 5 of the Wiking division saw their total strength radically reduced. The Panzer regiment was split up to help other units that were exposed which made the situation worse. The enormous Soviet offensive resulted in constant retreat and defensive fighting for the Germans troops who were hard pressed to repulse the constant Soviet attack. The Soviet attack continued up to October 31, when a considerably weakened Wiking crossed the Wisla river; this part of the front became relatively calm after this.

This makes 521 even more remarkable as pictures show it as having survived the brutal summer battle. By comparing pictures from before Operation Bargation and the ones taken in October 1944, it is clear that 521 had gone through repairs during this time where it received new skirt armour and a new rear stowage box that lacks Zimmerit.

It was not until the operation in Hungary in early January 1945 that the Wiking division saw action again. The last pictorial evidence that Mirko Bayerl and I have found show that Panther 521 may have made it as far as Hungary. The picture shows a burnt out tank with several of the features previously mentioned on Panther 521 such as cut front fenders and the "U" brackets on the engine deck. The burnt out wreck was photographed after the desperate break

out from the Jenö and Stuhlweissenburg cauldron, the crew were forced to abandon and destroy their vehicles in order to escape during the night of 22nd-23rd March 1945.

Building Panther 521

The original Dragon kit would need some adaption's to represent Panther 521. First of all the brackets welded on to the engine deck were tackled. I was Fortunate to obtain some brass strip that was sufficient which I soldered for better strength. I was not sure if they were welded on or bolted to the original tank. I assumed that they were welded so I made weld seams from Magic Sculpt that was textured with a syringe. The diagonally cut front fenders are "Part" photo etched fenders cut with a cutting wheel in my Dremel motor tool. The foremost side skirt plates also received the same treatment as they were a little shorter than the rest.

The Dragon kits comes with the weld seam pattern on the hull deck used on earlier production Ausf A's and Ausf D's. These are interlocked and I would need to modify them to represent the later straight cut edges and welds, so I started up my Dremel again and cut new straight edges to the armour plates. New weld seams were added with Magic Sculpt; this is a very tedious process but I am content with the result. I had wanted to portray the tank after the bitter summer fighting, this would mean adding a new rear stowage box without Zimmerit for which I used the "part" photo etched set. I used an Atak resin Zimmerit set to replicate the zimmerit on the vehicle.

I had decided to incorporate as many accessories I could find, and had already purchased all the necessary bits and pieces modellers so desperately need. Yes; I am aware of this 'super detailing syndrome' to get a vehicle to match reality which can sometimes get to absurd levels.

In my opinion, it is more important how well a model is painted, unfortunately, we often see a model with all the aftermarket bits and pieces added, but then inadequately painted. It therefore tends to end up as "just another model" despite the addition of enhanced detail. I will therefore just mention the detail parts that I have used and will not go in to a detailed description of each. The gun barrel is from Armorscale, WWII Productions tracks, Moskit exhausts, Eureka tow cables, Adler's Nest MG34 barrels and antenna and finally all photo etch is from the Polish manufacturer Part.

Painting the cat

It is rather fascinating to study all the different camouflage patterns used by the Wiking Division in the latter part of WWII. I am sure they were functional and from a modellers perspective it is more interesting to have all these patterns to choose from.

I prefer to prime my models with Chaos Black from the Games Workshop, which I find sprays evenly. Priming with black gives me two advantages: it hides some misfortunes from the building process, and it acts as pre-shading for the upcoming brighter colors.

This overview of the engine deck show the U brackets which can clearly be seen in the reference photos of 521. Other details such as the sledge, suitcase and jerry can were also added to make a more detailed impression.

I wait a couple of days to let the primer throughout dry, before applying the dark yellow with the airbrush. I used Tamiya paints, and for the Dunkel Gelb I mixed XF60 with a speckle of XF1, to make it slightly brighter. The black primer now comes very handy, as it appears as natural shades on the model. The camouflage on Panther 521 was applied in the usual free hand way, making it look rather blotchy. A close look at the pictures reveals a quite nondescript pattern, and this made me go for the same approach – free hand appliance in no particular pattern. Paints used for this was Tamiya XF 64 and XF 67 respectively. This was followed by dry brushing of each color with brighter nuances of Humbol paints.

Markings and weathering

I could not find any ready made decals for this particular vehicle, so I decided to use stencils instead. With the help of Stencilit products I made the number combination I needed. I also found that the stencils are more adaptable on uneven surfaces like Zimmerit. There is pictorial evidence that this tank had the divisional symbol on the front plate, so I did use an "Echelon" Wiking divisional sign for this. I used artistic license when I applied a decal on the gun cleaning rod tube though; as far as I know there is no established fact that this particular decal depicts the barely visible text on the pictures. Something is written on the cleaning rod tube, but I found it unreadable, and I later covered it with a sculpted soldier's jacket.

When the painting and marking was done, it was time for the weathering and washing to make it natural looking. This was done with washes of Winsor & Newton oil paints, to bring out details and enhance shades, together with pigments. Muddy areas like the idler wheels, were created with a mix of pigments, fine sand, static grass and white glue as adhesive that applied with an

old brush. I then went over the whole model with acrylic paints and pigments a few times, before I finished off the weathering with a thin misting of clear matte varnish to protect the paintwork and eliminate the inevitable shiny spots.

Figures

Making the base was a very enjoyable. I decided to make it as dynamic as possible. I chose to angle the tank diagonally and have a slight gradient to the right, the main gun was turned left to emphasise this even further. To recreate the Polish landscape in which the division fought, I had to show an open terrain with the characteristic fine sand seen in reference photos. This also made it logical to have the tank tilted a little. To avoid the classic 'tank-on-a-road-with-grass-on-the-sides' look, I made a considerable amount of Aber PE plants for a more varied and interesting vegetation combination. I scratch built a wooden fence to give some height to the vignette. The grass is linen cut to the correct length and then airbrushed with different green colours.

The base

Making the base was a very enjoyable. I decided to make it as dynamic as possible. I chose to angle the tank diagonally and have a slight gradient to the right, the main gun was turned left to emphasise this even further. To recreate the Polish landscape in which the division fought, I had to show an open terrain with the characteristic fine sand seen in reference photos. This also made it logical to have the tank tilted a little. To avoid the classic 'tank-on-a-road-with-grass-on-the-sides' look, I made a considerable amount of Aber PE plants for a more varied and interesting vegetation combination. I scratch built a wooden fence to give some height to the vignette. The grass is linen cut to the correct length

and then airbrushed with different green colours.

Conclusion

This project has probably been the most interesting one that I have undertaken. It was not the easiest and there were many days where I just sat and studied the reference pictures to see if I hand omitted any detail, or trying to figure out another way to replicate a particular part or detail. More often than not the pictures are blurry, out of focus or taken from the wrong angle to that needed to see a particular detail. Sometimes I had try to adopt logical thinking and exclude certain details, or as was the case with the front fenders, where I had evidence of them being cut on one side leading me to the assume that the other side was done the same way. This assumption turned out to be a correct, when Mirko Bayerl found the picture showing the burned out vehicle.

As I mentioned earlier, this project became much more exciting when I chose to build a particular tank, compared to build 'any' vehicle. I am sure there are faults or shortcomings on the model which I have not seen or been able to correctly verify, but I believe I ended up pretty close to the original.

Finally I would like to thank Mirko Bayerl for his invaluable help and sharing of his expertise in building Panther 521 from the Wiking division.

Markus Eriksson

References:
Panther Tank The quest for combat supremacy, Tomas L. Jentz, 1995, Schiffer Publishing Ltd.
SS Armor on the eastern front 1943-1945, Velimir Vuksic, 2005, J.J. Fedorowicz Publishing, Inc.
Warszawa 1944, Robert Bacyk, 2006, Leandoer & Ekholm Förlag HB.

The commander is a converted Pegaso figure, with a Hornet head and intercom set from Aber. The grenadier is a slightly modified Alpine figure. The camouflage smock was extended using Magic sculpt.

The reference pictures I had access to show that one of the stowage bins had been replaced as it lacks zimmerit. The photos also shows two buckets hanging from the exhaust pipes.

An overview of the driver and radio operator. The driver comes from Royal Model, with a Hornet head to add more character. The radio operator is a slightly converted Pegaso figure.

Note how the Panther follows a visual line along the fence and the grenadier pointing along the line of the barrel, giving a sense of direction and making the composition of the vignette more interesting. Note the vegetation that was carefully built up starting with the smallest roots and turfs, just like real vegetation. This is a detail often overlooked when making vignettes and dioramas.

221

PEIPER'S LETZTER SCHLAG

Peiper's Last Strike

Phil Stutcinskas returns with a atmospheric diorama set in the Ardennes offensive. Thorough examination of photos of Panther 221 resulted in a realistic copy of the original vehicle.

Inspiration - *Stimulation of the mind or feelings to activity or creativity.*

The inspiration for me to build models comes from a number of different places. A good quality model kit, An Interesting photo or story and probably the most inspiring thing for me, the visiting of a battlefield. For this diorama I was lucky to get inspiration from all of the above. I guess it started about 25 years ago when I first saw a picture of Panther 221 abandoned in La Gleize during the Ardennes offensive. Being a rare steel-wheeled version of the Panther G and the fact that it was a Kampfgruppe Peiper vehicle I found this tank very interesting.

The next piece of inspiration came from a book, "Duel In the Mist". This book is a treasure trove of information and photos about the actions of Kampfgruppe Peiper during the Ardennes offensive. It brought the history alive for me, telling the story of the battle for Stoumont in minute detail. The colour schemes of the tanks involved was also described in such a way that I had never seen before. The history and story behind Panther 221 was slowly coming alive for me.

Over the last few years, I have visited La Gleize and Stoumont in the Ardennes several times. For me, nothing is more stimulating and inspiring than walking and being in the place where the battles and history took place. Walking the largely unchanged streets really gets the imagination flowing. Plotting the positions of tanks and routes taken by the opposing forces one starts to get a picture and feeling of the battle.

Historical background

December19th, 1944. Stoumont 10.30 a.m. The battle for Stoumont Town was over. Kampgruppe Peiper had fought and won a bitter 3 hour fight against US forces. The surviving Americans had withdrawn down along the long winding N33 road towards Stoumont railway station. Peiper sent five

U.S troops examine "221" in La Gleize, Belgium.

of his tanks to pursue the Americans. In the meantime U.S reinforcements were being flung into the path of the advancing Germans and setting up positions around Stoumont Station. A 90mm M1 AA gun was set up behind the station covering a bend in the road some 300m away. The first tank to round the bend was Panther 222 commanded by SS Oberscharfuhrer Walter Ropeter. The tank was hit up to 9 times, setting it on fire. 3 of the 5 tank crew managed to bail out including Ropeter, who although burned, was saved due to him wearing a U boat leather uniform. Panther 221 commanded by Hauptscharfuhrer Heinz knappich was next in line and tried to get past the burning 222. Knappich's Panther was hit 8 or 9 times but unlike the previous Panther, this only resulted in damage to the frontal drive system. 221's part in the ill fated battle for Stoumont station was over. Knappich managed to withdraw and take the surviving crew members of Panther 222 back to LaGleize where the Kampfgruppe's field dressing station and repair facilities were positioned. Although not documented my diorama dêpicts Panther 221and the surviving crew being watched by the Kampfgruppe commander, SS Obersturmbanfuhrer Jochen Peiper as they make their way back to LaGleize.

By the end of the day, the Germans had lost the battle for Stoumont Station and that path of advance had been well and truly shut to them. Heavily outnumbered and running out of fuel and ammunition Kampfgruppe Peiper over the next few days would retreat back to La Gleize, being hammered by the now overwhelming US forces. Panther 221 made it back to LaGleize with the wounded crew. It took no further part in the battle and was abandoned on the 24th December when

John Florea/ Time&Life

This photo shows the scratch built figures which were carefully customized to fit to the vehicle´s engine deck and hatches.

221

the survivors of Kampfgruppe Peiper left La Gleize under the cover of darkness leaving all of their vehicles behind, many out of fuel and ammunition.

Modelling 221

The Panther model for this article was built by Roddy MacDougall using extensive references to ensure its accuracy in 2007. It sat gathering dust on a shelf until summer 2009 when he offered me the Panther to paint and include in this article. Please refer to Roddy MacDougall's build article on Panther 211 for a description of the work done and techniques used.

Painting 221

Each of the different Panther assembly plants started to apply standardised colour schemes to the vehicles in the fall of 1944. Furthermore, each assembly plant used different schemes and placed the Balkenkreuz in different positions. This means that vehicles produced by a certain assembly plant had a distinctive look particular to that factory. The steel wheeled Panthers produced by MAN were painted in a semi hard edged three colour scheme of red brown and olive green over a base coat of dark yellow. The wheels were a also a mixture of the three camouflage colours. An interesting feature of the MAN vehicles was the muzzle brake was left in the dark yellow base colour; this was due to the fact that the muzzle was covered during painting with a bag or cover. Many pictures of 221 exist so it is possible to work out many of the shapes or fields of colour on the actual camouflage pattern. I tried to replicate the pattern as accurately as I could by carefully examining the photos. The pattern was applied free hand with an airbrush over a base coat of dark yellow. This took quite a lot of time as the pattern was refined and altered many times, switching back and forth between the camouflage colours and the dark yellow base coat. By doing this, I could get the demarcation between the colours quite tight and neat. As for the weathering of 221, this was kept quite minimal as I reasoned the vehicle was quite new and therefore had not seen too much action. I believe the battle for Stoumont was the first and only combat 221 took part

Left side view of the Panther and it's crew before it was placed in the diorama.

in. The most difficult part of the weathering for me was the mud on the tracks and vehicle; it took weeks of trying different colours and washes. I found the portrayal of fresh mud quite difficult. I wanted to have a contrast between areas of fresh dark mud and lighter shades of dried mud. I was quite pleased with the result; it took a great deal of effort. Another aspect of the finishing of 221 that was tricky to replicate in a convincing way was the modelling of some pine tree boughs. I tried many different materials until I finally settled on some aftermarket material. Even this was quite difficult to use and I discarded most of it, just using a few select pieces. To make the pine boughs a little more convincing I painted the wooden branch areas in a greyish brow colour and drybrushed the pine needle areas with some pale green colour to bring out some of the texture.

Figures

Because I wanted to tell a story with the figure I had no choice but to do some extensive conversion and sculpting work, the figures of the two wounded crew members were the most extensive conversions. The heads and hands are stock aftermarket items and the rest of the uniformed areas were sculpted from Magic sculpt, some plastic figure parts were utilized too such as the boots. This kind of work takes many hours and cannot be rushed, the figures would be continually checked on the vehicle to make sure that the sit and look natural and correct looking. The crewman sitting in the rear escape hatch was a conversion of plastic kit parts and only required some minimal sculpting. However, getting the figure to sit in the hatch whilst holding onto the tank, proved quite difficult, I could not get the figures hands and clothes to interact realistically with the tank. I could not get around this whilst keeping the figure separate so I decided to sculpt and fix the figure to the tank before painting. This also meant that

the figure was painted as part of the turret. I found that this was the best solution to a tricky problem. The Knappich commander figure was straightforward in comparison. He is a Pegaso figure which I only had to alter a little in the hands and arms to get the pose I wanted. The figures on the back deck of the Panther took quite a lot of time and effort, but when a story is being told I think it is important to take the extra effort on them, especially as they will always be a focal point.

The Peiper figure along with the two accompanying soldiers on the other hand were straightforward to portray. They are from the excellent Alpine range of figures. All of the figures were painted with Citadel acrylics.

The Diorama

Right from the start of this project, I knew that 221 was going to set in a diorama. nothing paints or tells a story better than a diorama, it adds a sense of staging and drama to any model. Having visited the Stoumont and LaGleize area one quickly notices how hilly the area is. I was keen to portray this on the diorama by modelling the road on an incline. Also many houses in the area are made of a particular stone and have a distinctive look to the brickwork. I converted a Mini Art vac formed building that captured the look of the brickwork. The side steps and walls along with the footings were scratch built. The large tree in the middle of the diorama was a mixture of different pieces of roots and twigs carefully glued together with any gaps or missing areas being added and filled with magic sculpt. The whole tree structure was then textured with some acrylic filler and sealed with multiple coats of car primer to produce a tough structure. The leaves are silver birch tree seeds glued on individually using superglue . Like most things on this diorama this took many hours of work, but I think that it was worth the effort as the tree frames the diorama in a very nice way, especially as

The officers watching 221´s approach were taken from the Alpine range.

the ground work forms a sloped area. Modelling the groundwork of the diorama was pretty straightforward and fun to do. I guess that this was because I had recently walked and been around that kind of ground during the visits to the Ardennes. There is no substitute to actually seeing the real history and the places where those battles took place all those years ago.

My special thanks to Lester Plaskitt, Brian Murdoch, Kristoff Pulinkx, Johan and Herman Veurstaek for making the trips to the Ardennes such a memorable experience.

I would also thank Roddy MacDougall for his assistance with this project and Markus Lack for his help with the translation of the title.

Phil Stutcinskas

Documentation: Duel In The Mist

The front view of the Panther shows the battle damage on the front glacis.

PEIPER'S LETZTER SCHLAG

PEIPER'S
LAST STRIKE

Thank you for purchasing this book!

Please check our website for new releases.

www.canfora.se